A WOLF STORY

JAMES BYRON HUGGINS

HARVEST HOUSE PUBLISHERS
Eugene, Oregon 97402

A WOLF STORY

Copyright © 1993 by James Byron Huggins
Published by Harvest House Publishers
Eugene, Oregon 97402

Huggins, James Byron.
    A wolf story / James Byron Huggins.
      p.   cm.
    ISBN 1-56507-126-3
    I. Title.
    PS3558.U346W6   1993   93-10103
    813'.54—dc20   CIP

Printed in the United States of America.

For Karen
my wife
my friend
who endured everything
for love

About the Author

James Byron Huggins is a law enforcement officer who enjoys writing and photography. A journalism graduate, he once worked as a newspaper reporter. An avid backpacker and rock climber as well as the father of two, Byron and his wife Karen make their home in the southeastern part of the United States.

Book One

I only, am left;
and they seek my life,
to take it away.

o n e

Saul sensed death on the wind and stood to face his enemy. Old eyes, wise in years, scanned the surrounding woodline, reading every gentle movement of leaf and branch. Yet he saw no predator hidden within the swaying leaves. For a long moment he watched with keen brown eyes, searching, he felt, for ghosts. But there was nothing. The forest was as quiet as a grave. He rubbed his furry face with both paws, then raised his long ears and nose to the sky, knowing every scent, every sound. Uneasily he poised, tasting a fear he could not find. Then he slowly lowered his head, wondering.

Beneath the grassy knoll where he stood guard, the hare colony played and grazed in sleepy contentment. Saul shook his shaggy gray head. Was it his imagination? Was there truly anything to fear? He scanned the forest again, trying to peer through the green leaves into the dark woods beyond. But he saw nothing. He hesitated, doubting.

The colony seemed content and carefree, completely unaware of this strange sense of doom that hovered over him. Some were quietly digging for roots, though most were sleeping and resting beneath the warm sun. Even the Elders, gathering near the burrow hole, were sleepy with the day, seemingly unaware of any threat or danger.

Saul sat back upon his four paws, the points of his long ears descending to the ground behind his front shoulders, and sighed. Perhaps he was too old to be king, he thought. Soon it would be time to pass the burden of leadership onto younger, stronger shoulders.

Saul heard Windgate's heavy stride coming up behind him long before the burly hare arrived.

"How goes it, Saul?" Windgate laughed, resting his gigantic frame beside the old hare. "A good day, is it not?"

Windgate's broad, expressive face was dominated by two huge black eyes that hid nothing. His warm coat was dark, with small white dots running down his back. Saul harbored great affection for Windgate. The big hare was exactly what he seemed to be: large and lovable and easy to be with. Yet none was braver or quicker to defend the weak.

"We have a good life here in the field, far from wolf or man," said Windgate. "It was a good choice we made so many years ago to settle near the deep woods, eh? For myself, though, I think I've eaten too many berries!"

And laughing at his own joke, Windgate put a wide dark paw on Saul's shoulder, as friends would do. Saul felt the smile on his face. It was good to have a friend like Windgate, though he could be loud and boisterous and rowdy. But he was a true friend. If danger came upon them, this huge, clownish hare would be the first to stand in the gap. He had the heart of a king, never failing to embrace the sad or laugh with the joyful. And Saul had often wondered if Windgate would take his place in the pack one day.

Still laughing at himself, Windgate turned his funny, furry face toward Saul. "And why are you so sad, my friend? You have that old look in your eye. Do you see something? Is something there?"

"I always see something, brother," Saul replied. "Or hear something, or sense something. That is the burden of being king. But I'm not sure if anything is there. I have watched all day. And sometimes I think I see a shadow moving somewhere in the forest. But there is no sound, no scent."

Saul feared that his voice sounded frail with age, and weak. Consciously, he stiffened his shoulders as he spoke again.

"Perhaps it is nothing," he said, finally. "I don't know. But I feel . . . something. . . ."

Whether the danger was real or imagined, Windgate received the news with characteristic seriousness. In times of threat the burly hare was instantly transformed. Where there had been a smile, the dark face became menacing, a promise of deadly combat. His dark head turned rapidly to the surrounding woodline, and his broad, battle-scarred shoulders seemed to swell, challenging whatever would threaten the colony. Saul knew those wide, black eyes were swifter and sharper than his, and as he watched the dauntless head scan the forest gloom, he sensed that, among their kind, never had there been one greater in strength.

After a moment, Windgate shook his head.

"I see nothing, my friend," he said uneasily. "Perhaps something passed and now is gone."

"Perhaps," said Saul, but he did not relax. Somewhere, hidden within the shrouded forest, he sensed something more than darkness. But the signs were wrong. He lifted his head to watch the lofty trees. The sparrows and swallows continued their song. Squirrels leaped and danced in the swaying branches as lightly as the wind that swayed the gentle grass of the glade, where crickets carried their raking cry.

He gazed again across the glade, unable to lose his doubts. For despite the sunny calm, he felt a danger so real, so close. He hesitated sounding the alarm only because he did not wish to run from shadows. Nor did he wish for the children to see such a display. But there was something there . . . he knew . . . he felt.

"I will stay with you," Windgate added, settling in closer to Saul's gray mane. "And we will watch together for a while. Perhaps four eyes will see what two eyes cannot, eh?" And he laughed again.

Saul smiled and nodded, grateful for the company of an old friend.

Beneath the low hill where they watched, Thurgood
and DeSoto raced across the small field. The two little
hares were notoriously prone to trouble, sometimes by
chance, but mostly of their own making. They never
tired of playing, playing. Sometimes having so much fun
that they did not notice the open approach of danger.
But they were young. And they would learn. Saul
thought that it was best to let them enjoy the freedom
of youth before they assumed the hard burden of
guarding the colony.

DeSoto leaped into the air, swatting the top of
Thurgood's shaggy head with a yell, then tore off,
screaming, in a new direction. Thurgood gave chase,
laughing and grabbing at his friend.

Windgate shook his head.

"I cannot count the number of times we have saved
the lives of those two."

Saul laughed, despite himself.

"They are the reason we are here."

The big hare nodded solemnly, and the two rested in
silence. After a time the golden orb of the sun began its
slow descent, and the evening beamed with scattered
crimson rays. Touched by the majesty, Saul spoke, with
eyes that gazed beyond the glade and forest and sky.

"I was king before you were born, my friend, and I
have been king since. Over the long years I have taught
you the way of faith, by my example and by my words.
You know, as well as I, that we are children of the
Lightmaker. And you know that servants of the Dark
Lord hate us because our faith proclaims their doom. For

this they will destroy us, if they can. They do not grow weary of plotting against us. So we must never grow weary of guarding against them.

"That is why I have found great comfort in you. As an Elder, you have always been faithful, protecting the little ones. You have stood against foes far stronger that yourself, and but for the grace of the Lightmaker, you would have been destroyed. But he preserved your life so that you would do a greater work for him one day. Now, though, I feel the heavy weight of age upon me, and I sense the end of my days is near. When I have gone the way of all flesh, it will be time to choose a new king. I hope it will be you, my friend. Because you are willing to stand alone. You are willing to answer all the questions of the scornful, despising their scorn. And you are willing to die protecting those you love.

"Only remember this. Always the battle begins in the spirit, but it is war in every dimension of our life: spiritual, mental, and physical. And as in any real war, some of us will die in the fighting. So prepare yourself. Servants of the Dark Lord, in themselves alone, are strong. For flesh has a strength. But we struggle against more than flesh. We struggle against the Dark Lord himself, who never sleeps or rests."

In his hard silence, Windgate's head seemed framed by strength beyond flesh, his brow stern. He looked at Saul, grim and defiant, almost as if, even in this quiet moment, he was in some cosmic conflict with their unseen foe. Then the burly hare turned his gaze back toward the field, nodding solemnly. The sun continued its slow descent, and a heavy, unnatural cold began to fall while they watched together, on guard.

Mothers quietly gathering roots screamed as Thurgood and DeSoto catapulted across their paths, and an Elder raised a paw to swat the two ruffians as they hurtled past, causing Saul to smile at the antics. The old hare began to feel easier, more comfortable, even though the disturbing sensation refused to depart. Perhaps, he thought, he was simply too old to trust his instincts. Windgate was alert, yet sensed no danger waiting within the leafy gloom of the woodline. Saul wondered if the shapeless fears he sensed might not be the ghosts of battles past. He had learned long ago that some scars never healed.

Thurgood leaped on DeSoto's back, and they crashed headlong into a low stump. Then they were off again, DeSoto in pursuit, racing after Thurgood as he sped fast and low to outrun his pursuer.

Saul sensed the deadly shadow rising from the forest floor, even as the two hares neared the woodline, and his desperate cry of alarm shattered the quiet field. But it was too late. DeSoto caught his friend, leaping upon his back with a shriek and a furious tangle of legs, and the two disappeared into the green foliage.

"Get everyone to the hole!" Saul shouted to Windgate.

Windgate responded with a bellowing alarm.

Like a gray thunderbolt Saul hurled himself down the steep slope toward the forest. His grace and speed made lies of his years as the ground sped away beneath him, and his ears were laid back by a great rushing of wind. In seconds he was at the spot where the children had vanished.

Then, as his flashing legs brought him to the forest edge, he twisted to avoid a collision, for the young hares had burst free from the forest, faces white with terror, screaming in fear.

t w o

R un!" screamed Saul.

Then the forest wall exploded before a murderous impact, shredded beneath a monstrous beast that roared and struck in horrific rage. Only a desperate leap saved Saul as he threw himself to the side, narrowly evading its flashing fangs. He had no time to think, fighting frantically for balance, yet even in the frenzied encounter Saul sensed a power and rage beyond anything he had ever known, and glimpsed a glaring red eye that blazed with hellish hate.

Almost too quickly for the old hare to avoid, the jagged maw snapped for him again. Saul anticipated the attack and twisted violently to avoid the blow, but the beast was lightning. Sharp edges tore long burning furrows along the hare's side, and he was hurled, stunned and wounded, into a heap of boulders.

Roaring, the beast pounced toward him. But with

reflexes trained from a hundred fierce battles, Saul had already gained his feet. He leaped across the boulders, landing lightly at a distance.

Horrified, livid with fear and rage, Saul half turned in panic to flee for the forest. Then he realized he had to distract the beast for a moment longer so that the children could reach the burrow. And even with the thought, he whirled back to face the predator, his entire body electrified, prepared to evade its deadly lunge.

Horrible and malignant in the dying light, the beast did not hesitate. It moved after Saul with unnerving hatred, a rumbling snarl revealing two knifelike canines that extended to its lower jaw. And Saul knew his enemy.

It was a wolf. But not one of the ordinary, gray wolves that roamed the mountains of the North. This was a monster, a beast as much a creature of Hell as Earth. Saul had known its kind.

Head bowed and eyes glaring with demonic hate, it stalked forward. Bloodstained fangs hung distended and heavy with deaths of the innocent. Saul stared into the merciless eyes, caught the scent of the grave, and knew it was not hunger that drove the beast to kill. It killed only for the pleasure of killing. It was an evil servant of the Dark Lord, a creature that lived to destroy.

The dark wolf seemed to sense Saul's thoughts. Slowly, a hideous grin curled the cruel lips. Forest shadows, deepened by the descending sun, cast them into darkness. The beast halted a space apart, a silent laugh separating the deadly fangs. Then it lowered its black head and spoke.

"I have watched you long, Saul."

A voice of dirt shifting in the grave.

Saul involuntarily stepped back. He could only guess how long this beast had laid and watched, awaiting the chance to destroy his colony. Creatures such as this had infinite patience. For in their unholy allegiance to the Dark Lord, they had no higher purpose.

"I thought you had seen me," it intoned. "But you never sounded the alarm. Is that because you didn't trust yourself, Saul? Oh, yes, I know you. I know of the great Saul, King of the Colony near the Deep Woods. I have often wished to meet you so that we might . . . embrace."

Knifing wounds sliced through Saul's side, but he had recovered himself. His mind was detached, racing, measuring the distance between them and the surrounding rocks and trees. If the beast pounced again, Saul estimated that he had room for one desperate, evasive leap.

"You are not so wise, Saul. If you were, then perhaps both you and your colony would all be safe in their holes. But you are a fool. And you are weak."

A black tongue flicked out, tasting Saul's fear.

The old hare maneuvered for a more defensible position.

"What is your name, beast?" he said, stalling. "I know who you serve."

Dead eyes narrowed to black slits. "Do you think to trick me, Saul?"

Saul evenly held its gaze. "I trick no one."

"Yes. You trick me. But by now the little children are safe in the burrow. You have indeed saved them. Only you will die," it laughed. "But one dead servant of the Lightmaker is better than none. Your blood will satisfy me for the day."

Saul risked a glance toward the field. Yes, it was clear. All were safely underground. He had always known that death would come for him like this; he was only surprised that he had defied it for so long. But it was his place to face what his flesh feared to face, protecting those who could not protect themselves. And he had no regrets, for it was the highest service he could render to the Lightmaker. He steadied himself before he spoke, refusing to reveal the fear he felt.

"Then I will gladly die for those I love. I despise you. Do your worst."

The dark wolf's head tilted, a grin of amusement drawing forward the hideous jaws.

"Don't think to deceive me, Saul," it said. "I know you're afraid. And I am going to make you even more afraid. You are trying to be brave because you know I'm going to destroy you. But I am no fool, as you are. I don't believe you will live forever in some make-believe kingdom of the Lightmaker. Your faith is useless, Saul. Your faith did not save you from this. You serve a god who is weak, as you are weak. Whoever serves the Dark Lord lives by strength. We fear nothing. We take the Earth and destroy what we wish."

Carefully, slowly, Saul continued to inch away, subtly increasing the distance between them. Experience had trained him to always seek the tactical advantage.

"Useless words," snarled Saul, reacting as much against the creature's lies as its murderous intent. "Do you think I'm a child? Do you think I don't know the truth? I am King of the Colony near the Deep Woods, a servant of the Lightmaker. Your lies mean nothing to me. Your flesh is strong. But your days are short. I do not fear you. I will never fear you."

Stung, the creature moved mountainously forward, primordial, creating its own Night. Saul retreated, maintaining the gap as he spoke.

"Your doom is upon you, beast. You are deceived. Your master cares nothing for you. He will betray you in the end because you are worthless to him. His true battle is with the Lightmaker, and it is a battle he lost long ago. All you have is your flesh. But the spirit knows truth that the flesh will never know. And I will have victory over you in the end."

Though it had not increased its measured pace, the creature seemed to have slightly closed the gap. Saul backed into a boulder, adjusted, and quickly angled to another line of retreat.

"No, Saul, it's you who are deceived. The Lightmaker is defeated. And now my master awaits the extinction of your pitiful kind from the earth. You stand in the way of victory, Saul. So you must be destroyed. But before I destroy you, I will make you suffer. Yes, I will make you suffer long and horribly. And then, in the end, I will make you know such terrible pain that your feeble mind will crumble beneath me, and you will deny that you ever knew this accursed Lightmaker."

It laughed, scornful, and a cold wind rattled the leaves surrounding them. Carefully, so as not to trigger an attack, the old hare edged toward the dead trunk of an ancient oak.

"I only suffer because the Lightmaker has not yet ended your days, beast. I do not suffer because you rule the forest, or anything else. You rule nothing. I only suffer because I take a stand against you in the world. But even if you destroy me I will defeat you, because you're going to die, too. And then we'll stand together before the Lightmaker, who can choose between us."

Carefully positioning himself, Saul stopped his retreat. And the creature reflexively stopped its advance, confident in its strength, savoring his opponent's fear. The old hare crouched, subtly bringing his hind feet beneath him. Then he dug his claws into the soft forest floor, tensing his legs to leap.

"Oh, be assured," the dark wolf whispered, "there will indeed be judgment. And your judgment is death. Nothing will give me more pleasure than destroying you, your useless faith, and the children who would drag on your faith. And after I have destroyed you, I will give your bodies to the worms of the earth. I hate you, Saul, and all those like you."

An unearthly, volcanic rage smoldered in the dark wolf's eyes, and Saul saw the massively muscled chest breath once, deeply. It took all the old hare's control to still himself, waiting until the creature leaped upon him. Only then, he knew, could he make his desperate move. Saul hoped dimly that his powerful bound would carry him beyond reach of those murderous claws.

"You are weak, Saul," it rasped. "The Lightmaker is a dream. And the dream has ended!"

Instantly it was upon him, its thunderous roar shattering the night. Saul reacted like lightning, leaping in a high arch over the fallen oak. But even as he cleared the other side, a dark paw flashed toward him and a deadly blow struck him full in the chest. Saul felt claws tear deep, hot wounds across his side, spinning him through the air, stricken and torn, to crash brokenly against the ground.

Devastated by the cruel blow, Saul rolled numbly on the forest floor, struggling frantically for breath and consciousness. So powerful was the impact that for a moment he lost sense of time and place, gasping, only dimly perceiving where he was. As light rising slowly through a fog, his consciousness returned, and with it came the agonizing sensation of a mortal wound. Saul rolled dazedly onto his back, to behold a nightmarish shape looming over him. Foul breath descended.

"Killing you will be my pleasure," the dark wolf snarled, its eyes gleaming with an evil thrill. "I have won!" Hellish jaws shuddered, revealing jagged rows of fangs tinged with the blood of fallen foes.

Saul gasped for breath, speaking numbly. "I despise you, beast, but I pray for you. For the Lightmaker is coming... and your end... is near."

Only a brief moment did the dark eyes cloud, slavering jaws halting their descent. Then the black lips
shook, drawing back in a hideous snarl, and a rumbling
growl broke loose from deep in its cavernous chest. Saul
closed his eyes.

The intruder's bellowing yowl hit Saul's ears at the
same time that the furry shape hurtled through the air
to smash against the dark wolf's head. A long leg flashed
out, raking a bloody furrow across the beast's snout.

Stricken with rage and roaring in pain, the creature
snapped on empty air as the giant hare leaped away,
laughing. Saul was forgotten in the dark wolf's maniacal
rage as its bloodthirsty jaws snapped again and again
after the intruder who had launched this suicidal attack.

"Windgate!" Saul gasped numbly, shocked and dazed.
It took all his broken strength to rise from the ground,
yet he gained his feet in time to see Windgate disappear
beneath a bush. The black wolf leaped after him, unable
to reach within the thick branches.

"Ha!" Windgate mocked. "You may be ugly, but at
least you're stupid!"

In a flash Windgate raced from the bush and
burrowed beneath another one. The monster roared
savagely and leaped after him, deadly fangs missing the
soft fur by inches. Windgate shouted and taunted,
allowing the jaws close enough for a touch, but never
more. For all his burly size, the mocking hare moved
with blinding speed, never ceasing, never tiring. Within
moments he had lured the wolf deeper into the woods,
where it roared and struck demonically in its wrath.

"Hurry!"

Saul turned to the voice beside him. It was Benjamin, another Elder of the colony. Benjamin's old head, with his wild gray hair stuck out in all directions, appeared from behind a bush.

Numb from his wounds, Saul gasped, "I'll not leave Windgate alone!"

"Hurry, Saul! We have a plan! We won't leave Windgate to the beast!"

Saul heard Windgate dashing about, now here, now there. But he knew that the game would soon be up. If Windgate were left alone, eventually the beast would wear him down. But he also knew that his friend was too smart for a suicidal attack. Windgate would not have done this without a plan to survive. With a last quick glance, he turned and ran after Benjamin.

The Elder quickly led him across the field, halting in the middle. Saul could see that they were only a few feet from a well-hidden burrow hole. From a distance the wolf would not be able to see it. The beast would believe they were standing in the open field, far from the main burrow located on the far side.

"Now, stand up," said Benjamin.

Saul stood on his hind legs, sensing a gathering pain in his wounds with each passing breath, and felt blood seeping from his torn side.

"Aaaiiieeee!" Benjamin shouted across the field.

Within the forest gloom they saw the beast halt, red eyes glaring insanely out of the darkness.

"Here we are!" Benjamin shouted. "And we are not like him. We will fight you in the open! Come and face us, monster, if you dare!"

Only a frozen second did the wolf hesitate. Then Saul and Benjamin struggled to keep themselves still as it tore savagely free from the forest, leaving a gaping hole in the brushy wall. Face blackened even more in its rage, it hit the open field in a horrifying run, its long lean legs devouring the ground before it as it closed the distance with terrifying swiftness. Within seconds sure and certain death was nearly upon them, its nightmarish jaws distended.

Yet even as the dark wolf closed the final few feet, Saul saw Windgate's burly form running swiftly from the forest edge toward the burrow hole at the opposite end of the field. Then Benjamin threw himself down the hole with Saul beside him.

But the monster must have sensed the trick, for without missing a stride it turned, the dark shape sailing swift and low to cut off Windgate from the burrow hole. Windgate saw the creature turn toward him but did not alter his path. Now he was committed. He would reach the burrow ahead of the beast, or die in the open field.

Windgate hurled himself forward with every desperate flash of his long legs, while the dark wolf closed the remaining distance with supernatural speed. They reached the burrow together in a final, frantic leap. With all his great strength Windgate threw himself across the foaming fangs that seemed to snap shut around him. Then he was tumbling down the burrow hole, dazed but alive, as a thunderous impact blackened the sky above him and night descended in a demonic roar.

three

Deep beneath the grassy field, in the safety of the main hall, the colony huddled together and spoke in hushed tones. Children snuggled against their mothers, shivering and crying, and mothers whispered kind words to ease their fears.

Saul stood in the front of the big underground room and gazed affectionately at his people. It had been a narrow escape.

He shook his gray head as he thought of how close they had come to disaster. And he had even sensed the monster's presence. He closed his eyes and sighed. He was getting very old indeed.

He had sent Windgate back to the burrow in the hill above for a careful look. Perhaps the beast had departed. Yet Saul knew that now the beast would never stop his attack. It had become a battle to the death between the colony, which worshiped the Lightmaker, and this evil servant of the Dark Lord.

The Elders were gathered about Saul, their faces worried and distracted. They murmured amongst themselves, speaking in hushed whispers about the fearsome size and unnatural ferocity of the monster that had almost destroyed them all. Saul glared at them angrily.

"Is it defeat you speak of?" he demanded harshly. "If you will not speak of victory, then you will not speak! This is not a place for the weak of heart, or the fearful. Did the Lightmaker give us a spirit of fear or weakness? No. He gave us a spirit of courage and strength, to do what must be done. We serve the Lightmaker. And we will endure to the end. We're not going to tremble before any beast, Earthborn or Hellborn. Control yourselves. Be strong. Remember that the cowardly will not stand in the days to come. Nor will they stand before the Lightmaker. We will yet have victory."

The Elders lowered their heads quietly, and Saul stared at each of them in turn, allowing them to sense his courage, hoping they would find strength in his strength.

Windgate returned from the tunnel, breathing hard.

"It is not good, Saul," he whispered. "The beast . . . has begun to dig."

Saul's chest tightened with the news. It seemed that his wounds had opened again. Several of the Elders uttered low moans, and some whispered fearful prayers.

"Silence!" Saul said. "Do you wish to frighten the children even further?" He looked at Windgate. "What else?"

Windgate kept his voice low so that only Saul and the surrounding Elders could hear.

"Already it has moved several feet of dirt. We are safe for now. But by midnight it will be within the hall. I don't know what we can do. It appears strong enough to dig into all of the tunnels. There will be no place to hide."

Saul was silent, his face grim. He sensed a pale weariness, and lowered his head again, resting, speechless, waiting for his old strength to return. He prayed for wisdom, scanning the experiences of his long life for some tactic, some cunning, that would save them. But a disturbing cloud darkened his mind, a pervading sense of doom.

Old Benjamin spoke, as he was prone to do, talking to himself as much as to anyone else. "We could try to escape out the hidden door, but it would run us down ere we cleared the field. Or we could go up and fight it in the tunnel. But it would make swift work of us." His old eyes glared fiercely in the cavernous gloom. "'Tis a dark day visited upon us!"

Despite his pain and weariness, Saul smiled at the old hare. Benjamin had survived a hundred savage battles in his long life; battles against fox and dog, against rogue hares that attacked the colony, and relentless battles against the ravages of winters past. His gray mane was crisscrossed with the scars of combat, and his low brow reflected the hard suffering he had known. But he was not afraid. Benjamin's old body seemed to thrill with the challenge to defend his home. From beneath the heavy gray forehead, his dark eyes glinted defiantly.

"Do you not fear?" whispered Silas, a young hare who had only recently taken his place in the colony.

Benjamin threw him an angry gaze.

"I scorn my fear! I am a servant of the Lightmaker. I will put my fear into my claws! When the monster comes, I will be the first to face him. It is the Lightmaker who gives life. Who can take it from me? I will fight to the death to defend my home. That is the way the Lightmaker has ordained it. We do not surrender to evil. We do not lay down and die when death comes for us. We fight. We fight, because while we are of the Earth we must defend ourselves from creatures such as this. And in the end, if we die, then we die. Yet will I fight."

Shaken, Silas replied, "But how can we have victory over such a beast? It can't be beaten, not by force. We—"

"I will show you how to defeat it," Windgate broke in, his voice tense with anger. He raised his paw and flicked his claws. "By doing what we know is right. I do not need to decide whether it is right to defend my family. I do not need to think about whether it is right to save my friends. I know these things. The Lightmaker will grant us the strength to overcome, when we do what we know is right."

Saul leaned forward and calmly placed a paw upon his friend's shoulder, settling him. Then he smiled at his young champion, so quick to fight for those he loved. "We shall see what we shall do," he said quietly.

"But there can be no outrunning it," Silas said. "And there can be no fighting it. There is no hope. I am as willing as anyone to stand my ground. But we don't stand a chance. It is going to dig into our tunnels...," his voice trembled to conceal a desperate pitch, "...and nothing can stop it!"

Harsh voices stilled his debate. Silas, stung, looked about angrily for a moment, as if confused. Then he shook his head in disagreement, murmuring, and fell silent.

Saul gazed about him and measured the resolve he saw.

"Why don't we run out the back door when it runs in the front door?" sounded a small voice. Thurgood's frazzled head peeked around Windgate's muscular leg. "Yup, yup. That's what I'd do."

"What?" said Windgate. "Why, get back to your mother, young cub." He patted the youngster affectionately on the head. "This is not a place for you."

"Well, I'm not afraid!" said Thurgood, popping up to his full height, reaching almost to Windgate's hip. "And I say we run out the back door when he runs in the front. I ain't scared o' no wolf! Me and DeSoto already outran him once!"

Saul saw another shaggy head peek out from behind

Windgate's other side. The little hares looked at each other and nodded their heads furiously.

"Yup!" DeSoto said.

Thurgood stepped forward dramatically. "He don't talk much. But I do . . . ," he raised a finger for emphasis, "and I say—"

Windgate snatched both cubs from the floor by the scruff of the neck and lifted them aloft. Feet scurried frantically to escape but the effort only caused them to swing back and forth.

"We heard what you said," the burly hare spoke ominously, eyeing first one cub, then the other. Legs fell limp and they hung from his strong paws like leaves swaying in the breeze.

"Excuse me a moment," he said. "I have to take these two back to their mothers." And he disappeared into the back of the hall.

Silas leaned forward and spoke harshly toward Saul. "Foolishness!" he whispered. "We cannot outrun this monster. It would hunt us all down and kill us. It will never stop until we are all dead."

Benjamin spoke sharply. "If we listen to you, we will do nothing," he said. "But something must be done. We must fight or flee. There is no other choice. If we stand and debate, it will be upon us before the night is through. So we must decide. I, for myself and my family, vote to stand and fight. Some will surely fall. But perhaps we can convince this evil servant of the Dark Lord that we are not easy prey. I know of no other course. Silas is right in one thing. We can't run for the woods. Whoever runs will be tracked down and slain. There is no escaping the beast."

Saul listened intently and winced at the pain that lanced across his chest. Blood had matted to conceal the depth of his injuries, but he knew his wounds were serious. He sighed, feeling the sentence of death. So little time remained, so little hope. Yet hope and pray he must, if an answer was to be found.

Windgate returned.

"I have put the two little hooligans back with their mothers, where they belong. And I have been back up the tunnel."

"Yes?" said Silas. "It is gone?"

Windgate shook his head darkly. "It will be upon us by midnight."

Together they fell silent, each lost in his thoughts. Saul glanced somberly from face to face, sensing each hope, each prayer. Sadly, as the moments passed, he began to realize what he must do. Long ago, experience had taught him the last, most desperate defense. For in battle there was always one last move to make, as long as one still had life. It would be his final fight.

"My brothers, listen to me," he began, slowly and carefully. "It is true that if we run the beast will chase us down and kill us all. Not even you, Windgate, with all your courage and strength, are a match for him. But there is a chance we can survive. I was the one who stole the children from his grasp. I was the one who stood against him and defied the Dark Lord. So it hates me more than it hates you. And because of this hatred it will kill all of us, if it can. But I don't think it will.

"It is the Lightmaker who gives wisdom, so I assure you that we are wiser than this beast. And it is with wisdom that we will defeat it. You all know that servants of the Dark Lord pursue their own pleasures above all else. So that will be our weapon. We'll use the creature's own desires against him. We will give the beast something it wants. But what we give will cost him the treasure he desires most.

"Windgate, do you remember the great maze of caves we saw last winter, the one you said would be a fine home for the colony one day?"

Windgate nodded his stern brow.

"Then I will give the beast what it wants. And the price it pays shall be your lives."

Windgate spoke. "I don't like the direction you're going, brother. I don't intend to allow—"

Saul placed a paw upon his friend's hard shoulder.

"There's no other way, my friend. It is me he wants. He shall have me. But the chase will be long and hard, even for him. I will lead the creature far into the Deep Woods, farther than we have ever seen or gone before, where the snow lies deep and winter never leaves. I will take it to the place where the gray wolves roam. It will hunt me, and it will find me, in the end. But the end will be long in coming. And when the battle is done, you will all be far away to the south, in the caves by the brook. The beast may attack you again. But it will never be able to dig through the rock. And you'll have plenty

of food and water. As I lead him away, brother, you
must take the colony to the caves. That shall be our
new home. And if I escape him, I'll return to you."

Windgate only shook his head. "No. I can't allow
this. You are our king, so you must live. It is better that
I lead this monster on the chase. It is a race he will not
soon forget!"

Faintly, echoing through the hush of the tunnels, Saul
heard the scraping sounds of relentless digging. He knew
that little time remained. It was only Windgate's great
love that caused him to offer himself for the chase. Yet
this was a task for the old, not the young. For whoever
led the beast away would never return.

"The beast won't soon forget you, brother. But you
must do something that will let me reach the forest.
Without your part, I'll never get the head start I need to
lead it on the chase. And no one can take your place in
this. You alone can distract the creature long enough for
me to reach the woodline. Then with the moon, and
the stars, I will begin the final game."

Windgate's hard eyes grew even more indomitable,
refusing to allow Saul's sacrifice. Saul met his gaze, his
kingly head bent. For a long moment their eyes locked,
each unwilling to allow the other to forfeit his life.
Then, after a time, Windgate lowered his head, nodding
sadly.

Saul smiled. "One day you will be king," he said.

"Now, gather the little ones around me. For while we
still have time I will tell them a story that will always
give them hope."

Quietly the Elders gathered the mothers and children at the front of the hall. Saul stood before them, old and wise, his august head inspiring faith and strength to the weak of heart.

While far above them the sun was finally lost behind the distant hills, leaving only a golden glow upon the once peaceful field where nothing moved or lived except a monstrous black beast that ravaged the Earth and roared savagely in its demonic lust to destroy.

four

Silently and somberly the colony knelt before Saul, who knew this would be his last time to speak with those he loved. Perhaps, more than anything else, it had been this sadness that he had sensed all the day. He smiled gently. If it was necessary for him to die for his people, he thought, then so be it.

When all were settled and watchful, the old king raised his head and began to speak.

"Once all animals were one with the world, and we lived in peace with the wolf. It was a time without war or death. The wolf grazed with the ox, and the lion and lamb were friends.

"Then Evil entered the land. It came in the shape of a great black Beast who rebelled against the Lightmaker. It soared on wings of darkness, and lightning flashed across it, revealing the Hell within. It seemed as if the Earth cringed and pulled away from its presence. And

then it spoke, and the world was deceived. All were
touched by its evil. The forest was cursed, and
innocence was lost. For Evil had entered what the
Lightmaker had called Good. It was the first Dark Day.
Then the great wars began.

"Creature rose against creature. Wolf against wolf.
Each against his own kind. It was a time of great
suffering, a time of battle. Evil spread across the land
on the wind, and many worshiped it.

"But there remained one creature who was untainted
by Evil: a great Silver Wolf of awesome beauty and
majesty, who spoke of love and life, and who taught the
faithful to live as the Lightmaker intended, in hope that
they might one day make the world new.

"Eventually those who hated the Lightmaker gathered
against the Silver Wolf. They said he was evil. They said
he did not really serve the Lightmaker, and many were
deceived.

"Then the Dark Lord entered the land again, the
great Beast that rode the wind on black wings; a
creature of gigantic strength and gigantic rage. None
dared to stand against him in battle. He was without
equal, save for the Silver Wolf, who resisted him when
all others had fled in fear.

"They met at the forest edge. The Silver Wolf was
alone, and behind the Dark Lord roared a black tide of
evil that surged forward and back, waiting to claim the
dead body of the Lightmaker's most faithful servant.

"The Dark Lord blazed with the wrath of an ancient,
enduring evil. Though it was morning, the sun descended

and the sky was lost. The wind died, as if a grave had covered the land. And the Silver Wolf stood motionless, the last of the faithful, the one called Holy and True.

"The Dark Lord roared, and the land died. The trees withered and became skeletal sentinels, marking an endless tomb. The Beast seemed to grow even more monstrous in his wrath. His eyes became night, and his face grew darker than the blackness that surrounded him. Frost flowed from his gaping fangs, and he hovered over the Lightmaker's champion, a single silver shape against an endless sea of night.

"Then the cold and terrible breath of the Dark Lord descended upon the Silver Wolf, who surrendered his life to the grave.

"Even in death the Silver Wolf was more beautiful than the sun. His face still shone with light from within. And for a moment the darkness seemed to fall back from him, afraid to claim such a prize. Then the night swept over him and swept out again, casting his broken body on a dune of dry bones. And all the faithful who were left to mourn crept out of their hiding places and gathered together in one place, prepared for the final stand, now that their champion was lost.

"It was the Dark Night of the Soul, when the howling Beast was hot for the blood of the world. It was the great hour of sorrow that each of us must face in his heart one day, when the world is dark and the battle seems lost; the hour when strength has fled and only hope remains.

"Evil rolled forward in an endless sea, intent on destroying the faithful. The strongest held the front, so the battle was fierce. Yet the Dark Lord led a force greater than any that walked the Earth, and the good were falling, a promise of death sweeping over them, a whisper of the grave on the wind. And then the morning dawned again.

"It came as lightning, not as the slow slanting of morning rays at the first light of day. No, with this morning the hills were suddenly white with light, and the forest trembled as if it realized something that the wolf and hare were yet to know. Then the faithful saw the sight of sights, the hope of hopes, the promise of a new day.

"On the wings of a great white cloud came the Silver Wolf who had been slain, the Lightmaker's faithful one. Yet he was no longer silver, but white: whiter than the great white bear that roams the ice, whiter than the snow that covers the forest in winter, whiter than the new morning sun that chased shadows from the land. And the Dark Lord saw him and was terrible in his wrath. The Beast rose into the air on great black wings, his face a mask of horror and death.

"The White Wolf rose on clouds of light, and the light fell across the hills and dunes of bleached bones where the faithful had been slain. And the bones rose from the dead and took shape behind the White Wolf to become a surging white sea, prepared to make war upon the Night.

"They met in the sky above the Deep Woods, two endless shapes battling for the fate of the world. The Dark Lord breathed frost upon the White Wolf, and his breath was Winter and Night and Death. The forest fell cold as the grave, and the mountains crumbled into dust.

"Then the White Wolf laughed, and the curse was broken. The land was warm again, the trees green with spring. The hills became alive with rose and gold, and mountains took shape and burst from the earth like giants rising from the grave. It was laughter that threw light into every corner of the land, laughter that made the rivers break forth from the dry earth and flow fresh and blue once more, laughter that healed the brokenhearted and the sick, and laughter that gave strength to the weary. Then the stars blazed in the noonday sky, brighter than any star that ever blazed at night. And the eagle, hawk, and dove took to the air and became a white soaring tide behind the White Wolf.

"Then the White Wolf told the Dark Lord that when he had killed the Silver Wolf, he had killed an innocent creature. The Dark Lord had held the right to kill those who were touched by his evil, those who no longer belonged to the Lightmaker. But the Silver Wolf had never been touched by evil. And when the Dark Lord killed him, an innocent creature, he condemned himself and his legions of darkness forever.

"And now, said the White Wolf, because of the Silver Wolf's innocent death, all creatures who wanted to be reunited with the Lightmaker could do so because of his sacrifice.

"Then the White Wolf told the Dark Lord that one day he would be utterly destroyed by the Lightmaker for the evil he had done. But until that final day, the Beast would be allowed to roam the earth.

"Then as a wolf will shake a rat, the White Wolf shook the Dark Lord and ascended more quickly than an eagle to the heights where only the stars dwell. And with a cry that reached to the earth again, he cast the Dark Lord down.

"As the Beast plunged to the land, his roar of rage was thunder and the terror of his fate transformed his shape. He was consumed by fire, his body scorched like blackest night to mark his soul. The land trembled when he crashed into the forest gloom, and he was heard no more.

"The battle won, the White Wolf returned to the faithful. He spoke of many things: of love and life and the promise left to keep. He spoke of laughter and the morning and a new birth awaiting. And he spoke of faith and the power that would overcome the Dark Lord. And these are those things that we are always teaching you, our children.

"Then the White Wolf told the faithful that he had to leave them for a time to return to the Lightmaker. But, he said, on some faraway morning, when the world had passed through the night, he would come back; and when he did, the forest would once again be made one.

"'But until I do,' he said, 'you must be on your guard. For the Lightmaker will allow the Beast and his servants to roam the Earth. These Dark Ones will make war upon you, deceive you, and frighten you. So do not grow weary of watching. And do not fear the evil ones, for by my spirit within you, you shall overcome them. Only remember: be strong, be courageous, do what you know is right. And I will be with you forever.'

"Then, ascending into the morning, the White Wolf was lost in the Light."

five

All heads were bowed as Saul fell silent. Then, quietly, each turned and moved toward the back of the hall until only the guardians of the pack remained with the old and wounded king.

Saul raised his head.

"Now, my friends, is the hour of darkness. Remember, in times to come, that your greatest battles will always be fought in the night, when you feel cold, afraid, and alone. But you are never alone. You will have little hope for victory, but you must never surrender your hope. Endure the struggle, endure it all to the end. Because no night will last forever. Always the morning comes. So keep your balance. All of life comes back to this: you must stand by faith, despite your suffering, despite your pain. Endure until there is nothing left to endure. And you will overcome, in the end."

Saul turned toward Windgate.

"But now we must do battle in the flesh to defend our home. And hell holds no fury such as we will unleash. Windgate, you and Benjamin must go up into the tunnel and fight the beast, distracting it while I escape out the hidden burrow and run for the trees. When I reach the forest edge, I will call to the wolf and lead him on the chase. And when you are certain that he has followed, lead the colony south."

Windgate nodded, his eyes flashing. For a moment the big hare seemed transformed, almost more than flesh, as he looked at the old king one last time. Then, impulsively, Windgate smothered Saul in a rocklike embrace. Only for a breath did they stand; then the big hare separated, holding Saul with his steady gaze.

"I won't fail you," he whispered.

Without another word Windgate turned and bounded into the main tunnel, Benjamin close behind. And Saul ran toward the back of the hall, entered the rear tunnel, and raced through the dark corridor toward the hidden burrow.

As Windgate neared the mouth of the tunnel, he could feel the tremors from above. He crept steadily forward until he could see black claws scraping mechanically at the earth, shoveling clouds of dirt behind the monstrous form. The beast cursed and snarled, and did not seem to notice his approach.

Windgate halted just below the tunnel mouth. And as a large paw stretched out to move another chunk of earth, the fierce hare leaped forward, slashing open a gash on the lean foreleg. Almost before he struck, Windgate had stopped his forward momentum and had begun to leap back again. He was already frantically scampering out of range before the monster felt the blow. Even so, in a lightning-quick response the savage jaws snapped shut inches above his head.

"Missed me again!" mocked Windgate. "Shall I slow down for you?"

The reply was a thunderous roar and a long foreleg that blasted down the tunnel, missing Windgate by a hair. The beast groped blindly, unable to peer down the blackness of the tunnel, and Windgate bit down viciously on the wide paw. His attack brought an angry snarl from the gaping jaws and a cry of battle from Benjamin, who leaped forward, slashing furiously.

On the other side of the field, Saul emerged from the hidden burrow. He saw the dark outline of the monster digging fiendishly at the main tunnel, and he raced stealthily for the treeline. He crossed the field low and quiet, using the swaying grass to conceal his careful movements. For a moment he could hear Windgate's taunting laugh and the dark wolf's snarling, then pandemonium broke loose at the tunnel entrance.

Without thinking Saul cast a quick glance over his shoulder and saw that a large section of earth had suddenly collapsed, leaving Windgate and Benjamin exposed from above. The dark wolf howled gleefully and leapt upon the unprotected figures. And before he realized what he was doing, Saul had stopped in the open field, staring distraught at the evil misfortune. He hesitated, began to run to assist his friends, but realized even the three of them united would die quickly in open combat against the beast. Quickly he turned and raced, all care forgotten, for the forest edge. If he could reach the woodline in time, perhaps he could yet draw their enemy to the chase.

At the burrow, Windgate felt the massive mantle of earth collapse, crushing him against the ground, and knew instantly what had happened. Even as the bloodstained snout descended toward him, Windgate reacted with a savage roar and explosive effort that threw off the crusted shelf. Jagged edges struck him in the chest, but it was a glancing blow. Then the big hare felt a tearing wound in his shoulder, and he was hurled backward, a lean foreleg pinning him down.

Black breath fouled his face.

"You are the one," it rasped viciously, almost laughing in its glee. "You are the one who rescued your king. Oh, I shall enjoy this."

Its fangs snaked out, slashing Windgate's shoulder again. Then it looked him in the eye and gleamed.

Windgate's fierce scowl hid any signs of pain.

"You will not show pain?"

The beast placed a wide, black paw upon Benjamin, who was just struggling free of the dirt shelf, and crushed down. The old hare yelled out but was held motionless against the ground.

"Perhaps I should crush him like a worm?"

Windgate was prepared to die, and he knew that Benjamin was also prepared to give his life so that Saul could reach the woodline. He would give this monster no pleasure.

"I despise you, beast," said Windgate. "I serve the Lightmaker! If we can't defeat you, then he will send someone who can!"

The dead black eyes laughed.

"You believe there are any in the forest who will face me? I rule the Night! The Dark Lord has given me the strength and power. Know that as I destroy your flesh."

Only a fleeting glimpse alerted Windgate to the tiny shadows racing up the tunnel beside him.

"No!" he shouted as Thurgood and DeSoto exploded from the tunnel entrance, bellowing war cries.

"Aaaiiieeee!" screamed small voices as the two tiny figures leapt into the fray, even as Benjamin savagely threw off the wolf's paw and tore free of the dirt shelf.

Thurgood and DeSoto separated and dashed frantically down both sides of the monster, but the flashing fangs followed, easily catching Thurgood by a rear leg. The little hare cried out as the jaws snapped shut. And DeSoto, electrified at his friend's cry, spun in stride and sank tiny teeth into a brutish black leg.

Thurgood cried out again, and DeSoto was hurled backwards from a savage kick to smash stunningly against the tunnel side. Time seemed to stand still as Benjamin launched himself toward the hideous head, bellowing his battle cry, and Windgate crouched, bracing himself for a single, daring move that would save or doom them all.

Benjamin collided against the dark head and slashed above a glaring red eye with his claws. The wolf winced at the blow, released Thurgood, and raised itself onto its hind legs. A lean foreleg slashed through the air, striking Benjamin in the shoulder. And then Windgate moved, with a powerful bound and his forelegs extended for a deadly embrace of the monstrous head.

"Get Thurgood!" Windgate cried as he collided with the wolf's head, sinking teeth deeply into its brow and digging claws high into the face, far from the tearing jaws.

Instantly the dark wolf reacted, roaring, insanely clawing at the burly hare and shaking its head frantically to dislodge its foe. Only Windgate's colossal strength kept him above the snapping jaws as the creature raked deep furrows down his back. The big hare desperately dug deeper into the hideous brow, determined to hold the beast long enough for Benjamin to rescue the children.

Benjamin crashed against the ground, stunned and dazed. He was in no pain at all, so great was his wound. His shoulder was slashed open to the bone, and his feet were sluggish to respond. But he had suffered many deadly wounds in his long life, and he knew from experience that he could still move. His indomitable will strengthened his body, forcing it to respond. Clumsily, he rose and staggered to Thurgood, who was quiet. Benjamin saw in a glance that he was still alive; he had suffered a mangling wound, but would heal in

time. Forcing his legs to respond, he dragged the still
form into the burrow.

"Hurry!" Benjamin shouted to DeSoto, who followed
behind, pushing on Thurgood.

Together they tumbled down the tunnel, and
Benjamin cast a last wild look over his shoulder to see
the horrific black shape raised against the night sky,
savagely shaking its head and snapping fiendishly at the
strong legs that raked its face.

Windgate knew he could not hold on much longer. A
frantic glance told him that the others had found
shelter, and he knew that by now Saul would have
reached the forest.

Then, in a last desperate effort to dislodge its
attacker, the wolf lowered its head and slammed him
into the dirt wall. Windgate bellowed in pain and almost
lost his narrow hold. His claws dug deeper into the
bloody wounds, and he fiercely bit again into the hairy
forehead.

The wolf howled and shook its head.

Saul reached the forest edge to see the dark wolf
shaking and snarling maniacally. And as its massive
head passed over the tunnel entrance he saw Windgate's
burly form fall from the dark shoulders, descending to a
place directly in front of the tunnel entrance. Almost
before the monster realized that his punishing foe had
dropped, Windgate had landed. And in a flash the hare
scrambled back, disappearing down the entrance.

Saul only dimly noticed the warm blood seeping from
his wounds. It no longer mattered, he thought, as he

gazed down in the moonlight at the spreading black stain. He knew his time had come.

"Soon, it will be over," he said weakly.

Rising onto his hind legs, he faced the glade that he had once called home.

"Turn and face me, monster!" his voice echoed across the field of battle. "Turn and face the one who escaped you! I was the one who snatched the children from your grasp and mocked you in the forest. I was the one who led my colony against you. And I will be the one who leaves you dead by the dawn! Turn and fight me, if you dare!"

Saul looked long enough to see the dark shape hurtling across the field, the long legs devouring the distance between them with incredible speed. Then he turned and raced into the woods, running left, then right, then left again. He heard the creature crash into the forest edge and hesitate, confused at his direction. And silently, with all the skill and cunning of his years, Saul began to pick a careful path into the Deep Woods.

Behind him, a dark cloud hovered over the face of the beast. Red jaws thirsted for the blood of his foe, the one who resisted him. For a long moment it searched the woods with hungry eyes. It would usually hunt by sight. But the old hare was cunning. He would make no sound and leave no sign.

The beast poised in the night, angry and confused. Then a familiar scent reached out, the scent of a dying foe, and the blood he shed. Bending its gigantic black head, the dark wolf found the faint trail, the life and death of his enemy. Grinning hideously, eyes flaming with hate, it moved slowly forward, following the thin, scattered droplets of blood through the blackened forest as surely as a river.

s i x

A silent wind swirled snow and fallen leaves across the forest floor, through haunting shadows cast by a haggard moon and past a silver wolf that sat motionless beside a wide, white glade of snow and ice.

An arctic storm had descended on the dying sun, leaving the forest a white landscape etched with skeletal silhouettes and darkened pits of gloom. And already snow was climbing in an icy tomb at the young wolf's feet, as if seeking to bury him here, within the storm, in these ghastly, nightmarish woods.

In the silver wolf's mind it seemed that even the dark, swaying trees had taken on terrible life and would reach down to tear and rend him. Only the knowledge that his tracks through the forest were hidden beneath the falling snow gave him comfort. For he knew that even the beast he might face tonight could not destroy what it could not find.

Fearfully, as he had done since darkness descended, the wolf searched the distant treeline, half-hidden in the swirling storm. A relentless terror seemed to cripple his strength, even as ice coated his silver mane. Mechanically he swung his gaze back and forth across the forest glade, searching the mist that had brought the snow. He knew that if death came for him tonight, it would come out of the storm.

Yet despite his wasting fear, the silver wolf knew he could not leave this lonely place until the morning sun dawned golden on the glade before him. For tonight was the Watch, the Ritual of Power, when a young wolf spent his first night alone in the Deep Woods, without the protection of the pack.

It was the hour when he must prove himself worthy of leadership if he would gain his rightful place on the Council. Yet it was a dreaded test, and the silver wolf had lived in fear of it, for he knew that servants of the Dark Lord roamed this cursed forest at night. And those who worshiped the Dark Lord were eternal enemies of his pack, the gray wolves who roamed the North and worshiped the Lightmaker.

"I am Aramus, son of Gianavel," the silver wolf said softly to himself. "I won't be afraid."

Yet his heart chilled when he imagined what might come for him before the dawn. And only his great love for Gianavel, his father who had long been king of their kind, gave him strength. For he found no peace in the

Old Story, or the Promise of the White Wolf. He
believed in the Lightmaker, who had created the world,
but his faith had never given him victory over his fears.

Hunching forward, Aramus lowered his head against a
blast of freezing air that sliced through his thick fur.
And he remembered another night not so long ago, in a
forest far from this lonely place, where he had first seen
the enemy of his pack, that dark destroyer of lives. For
the horror of that sight had forever scarred his heart. . . .

♦ ♦ ♦

It had been a good day for the males of the pack, a
day of hunting and playing, and the Elders had run
ahead to scout for fresh trails, leaving the young wolves
alone in the night, listening to the distant howls that
slowly ranged across the hills and then turned toward
them again. It was a time for frolicking in the snow,
wrestling playfully in tests of strength. And the
surrounding forest had been forgotten, along with the
death that walked its darkened corridors, when suddenly
the night about them grew eerily still.

In a single breath the young wolves sensed the deadly
change and fell silent, searching the night for sight or
sound of an enemy. And even as they raised their heads
to test the air, the scent of something strange and
hideous reached them on the wind. With the first faint
smell, they tasted its hate. And swiftly, silently, they
huddled together, afraid even to breathe. The forest
about them became heavy and cold as a tomb. Then the

scent grew stronger, as if some ancient abomination had stepped forth from its hellish grave. And the wolves shivered, shoulder to shoulder, listening anxiously for the howls of their fathers approaching.

Darkness fell so thick that Aramus could barely see beyond the trees that enclosed him, but he did not need his eyes. He knew the beast was already beside them in the night, so near he could feel its black breath warming the arctic air. The young wolves trembled with fear, and Aramus searched the night with wide eyes, dreading what he might see.

Long moments passed, and the scattered howls of their fathers grew nearer. Then, from within the shadows, Aramus saw something emerging from the forest gloom, a nightmarish face of dark flame framed by Night.

Shrouded by living darkness, a pair of hungry eyes peered at him for a long moment. Then slowly, more horrible than the malignant stare, a grin of jagged jaws spread beneath. A long time the ghastly sight was poised in the night. And Aramus caught the shocking scent of something dead, or living in death.

Suddenly the Elders broke into the nearby clearing at full cry. The malignant, sinister eyes blinked angrily, hesitating, and then vanished. Aramus sensed the thing pass close beside him as it moved deeper into the shadowed forest. And as surely as he breathed, he knew that here was a beast who lived only to slay the living.

When the Elders had rejoined them, the frightened young wolves excitedly told their fathers of the harrowing ordeal. Gianavel, Aramus's father, listened patiently

as his son spoke, his deep gray eyes unreadable. But the
old wolf would sometimes turn his massive head, glaring
into the darkness, as if challenging what dwelt there.
And as Aramus finished his tale, his father turned to
him again.

"I know this one," Gianavel spoke slowly. "He is an
old and evil wolf. His name is Baalkor, and he has slain
many of our kind. He is a sworn enemy of all who
worship the Lightmaker. If we hadn't returned, he would
have attacked you. But even Baalkor is no match for the
strength of the pack, so he fled."

Aramus glanced fearfully at the forbidding forest.
Every shadowed pit of the betraying darkness seemed to
conceal that unearthly beast, its nightmarish shape
hidden . . . waiting.

Then he heard Gianavel's commanding voice speaking
again.

"There are still some things I haven't told you about
the Dark Lord, my son. You know already that many
have surrendered to the darkness. There are wolves and
lions and countless other beasts who make war against
the Lightmaker. But now, I see, that the time is upon us
when I must tell you more.

"All those who worship the Dark Lord are led by an
evil alliance of three, known as the Dark Council. And
it has sworn eternal war against all who worship the
Lightmaker. Baalkor, the black wolf, is one of the
Council. Second among them is Incomel, a cruel
mountain lion that has long ravaged the land. And

chief of the Dark Council is Corbis, a godlike beast of a bear, supreme on the Earth in strength.

"Baalkor was once the strongest of our pack and roamed the mountains of our homeland. Long ago, when I was young, as you are, I hunted beside him. But when he reached the age to endure the Watch, he turned away from his faith to pursue the pleasures of the Night, rebelling against the Lightmaker to worship the Dark Lord. Since then, he has slain many of our kind. Years ago he hunted down our beloved king, Karidural, and killed him in the Deep Woods. And as you know, upon Karidural's death I was chosen king.

"Soon after, Baalkor hunted me down also, when I was alone in the frozen North. He trapped me on a ledge of ice and demanded that I swear allegiance to the Dark Lord. But I told him that I was a servant of the Lightmaker. 'Always,' I said, 'I stand between you and the world.'

"We fought through the long night, with only the stars to see the savage outcome. I did not ask for mercy, nor did I give any. The ledge was torn and bloodied by our struggle, and today I bear the scars of that conflict. Then with morning the ravaged ice collapsed beneath us, and we tumbled together into the White River. Even as we fell, we fought, taking the battle to the death. Then we crashed together into the swirling waters and were separated. When I reached the shore he could not be seen. But I knew that he had survived. He had escaped me to attack me on another night when I would be low in strength. And that is how he will attack you."

Aramus stared into the night. His legs still trembled from his ordeal, and he stiffened them to conceal his fear.

"If you defeat him," Gianavel continued, "he will retreat. But he will always return. On another night, when you are tired, weak, or afraid, he will come to you again. He will wait until you are beaten down by the world, attacking when you are weary. He will lure you with pleasures and the secret desires of your heart. It will be a great struggle. But you must endure it. You must endure. The Lightmaker will not allow you to suffer more than you can bear. Always, his grace is sufficient for the task.

"Remember this, and it will give you hope. And when your great suffering has ended and you stand again in peace, then you will possess a deeper strength and understanding. You will be more than you were. And your heart will be great, guiding you with wisdom and knowledge."

Often, his father had spoken of the spirit, the endless need for strength and faith, and being set free from the world. But Aramus had never really understood the old wolf's teachings. Always, it seemed, no matter how faithful he tried to be, his fears defeated him.

Now his father looked upon him, noble and wise. And no trace of disappointment could be heard in the soothing voice as he spoke again.

"I know you don't understand now, my son. But the time will come when the Lightmaker will enlarge your heart, renewing all that is within you, making you strong with his strength. And then you will see, even as I do."

His father's kingly head turned again toward the darkness, and Aramus knew that nothing could hide the dark wolf from those piercing gray eyes. After a moment the eyes softened, looked upon him once more.

"Do not fear Baalkor," his father said, smiling. "Death and the power of darkness have been conquered. You are a child of the Lightmaker, and there is nothing that Baalkor can take from you."

Yet Aramus found little comfort in his father's words. He only remembered the nightmarish face poised in the night, and he stared silently into the shadows, ashamed to admit his fear.

Gianavel smiled gently, and the shadows seemed to retreat from his presence. The majestic voice was strong and clear in the night.

"The battle is beyond the flesh, my son. Our victory has already been promised, an end made sure. Cling to what you have learned, and it will be life for you when death is near. Be strong. Be courageous. Do what you know is right."

They had returned home in silence that night, Aramus lost in his thoughts. He had traveled close to his father's side, thinking again and again of the malevolent red eyes and hideous face grinning at him from the stygian night. His faith seemed broken, shattered. He wondered if he would ever have the strength to face his fears.

◆ ◆ ◆

Saul ran now with less caution. His old legs were heavy, and the cold air tore at his ravaged lungs with each ragged breath. Deeper and deeper he had fled into the woods, feeling the darkness thicken, as if the night itself were alive and battling in concert with the creature that chased him. He stumbled over rocks and branches, bruised and shaken. He tumbled painfully over ledges that descended into pits of gloom, running, always running.

The cruel air was colder with every step he took toward the deepest part of this cursed forest. It was farther than he had ever been before. Already he had run for hours through the darkness, using every trick he possessed to confuse his enemy. Three times he had descended into freezing waters and let them carry him downstream. The shock alone had almost killed him. But he had forced himself to remain in the flowing channels until he felt a deathlike cold in his heart. Then he had numbly climbed onto the opposite bank, picking a careful trail, doubling back and circling again in a desperate attempt to confuse his enemy, his strength failing more with each step.

Then, as Saul crept from the final, freezing stream, the arctic air swept across him with killing cold, stiffening his damp mane with ice, and he knew that he had reached the heart of the Deep Woods, where winter never leaves. It was the land of the Dark Lord's servants. Now it was tracking him in the forest it knew best. Saul realized that in this evil land there would be no tricks that could deceive that destroyer of lives. But he would never surrender. He would struggle against his persecutor until it fell upon him in its unholy rage, and then, too, he would resist. Though Saul had not heard its infernal howl for several hours, he sensed that it had not lost his trail. It was hunting him with ancient patience. And it would find him, in the end.

Saul hesitated at the crest of a thorny hill. His old body, slashed and beaten, was failing. He had struggled to run faster, but his legs lifted more painfully, more slowly, with every step.

He gazed behind him into the darkness and sensed the evil presence tracking him through the night. For a moment he stared into the gloom, but the last of his fear was quickly disappearing. No longer did he look only into the night. For in the passing hours he had begun to sense a new land, where stars shone eternal and green hills rolled forever, a land he had always hoped for, and awaited. As he rested, a silent sense of love warmed him, and he knew that the Lightmaker had not left him alone, even in this terrible hour.

Saul lowered his head, breathing heavily, perceiving that he was only struggling out his part in some drama that had always awaited him. Somewhere, in the dim recesses of his mind, Saul had anticipated this moment all his life. Raising his head, he gazed quietly, hopefully, at the stars.

His flesh was hardening with frost, and stabbing pangs of agony made his breath pale and weak. Yet Saul felt strangely alive, ready to fight to the death.

The stars are so much like us, he thought. Bright and beautiful, full of wonder and light, yet surrounded by such terrible darkness. And even so, the darkness cannot overcome them, for they shine on and on through the painful night, casting light for all the world to see.

Saul smiled weakly, praying, hoping that the Light-maker would be pleased with him when the battle was done. Then he staggered down the hill toward a wide, white glade.

Slowly at first, snow began to spin swirling patterns across the old hare's path. Saul limped on through the mist, resisting the deathlike weariness that crippled his body. The storm continued, gathering strength. But still he pushed defiantly onward, refusing to lie down and allow the hateful night to force a swift and cruel ending to his pain. Finally the storm lashed across him with demonic frenzy, crushing him with sheets of ice and swirling snow. Ice coated his chilled gray fur and numbed his strength. Yet still he stumbled blindly forward, sensing his own death, leading the beast onward with the last, undying flame of his will.

seven

Lost in the memory of that dark night,
Aramus was returned to the storm by
slashing ice. The assault penetrated his thick coat,
chilling his bones with hateful cold. In defiance he
shook his head violently, splashing moonlight in a white
shower of snow.

He raised his head to watch the dark swaying trees
whispering their ancient song. Aramus had not spoken a
word to his father on the long day's journey from their
mountain home to the Deep Woods. And finally, when
the majestic gray wolf had left him alone, to return in
the morning, Aramus had become still as stone, watching the shadows grow long and deep and cold. He had
known every whisper of leaf and bush, caught the scent
of all that moved in the south, where the wind was
born. And as the night had slowly passed, he had begun

to feel a thin sense of safety, for he sensed that no
creature moved or lived where he rested now.

In the morning, after his father returned for him,
they would begin the long journey north to their
mountain home. But first he must survive the night.
And it was not just the darkness he feared. More, he
feared Baalkor, the beast that had passed him in the
night not so long ago. Aramus's blood chilled at the
memory of that nightmarish face poised in the
shadows—grinning, tasting his weakness.

Then, as he had done a hundred times, Aramus
lowered his head against a freezing blast of arctic air that
rushed across the glade like the deadly breath of some
evil, ancient beast. And when the crippling cold had
passed, he raised his eyes again to search timidly along
the faraway treeline, his mind beginning to crumble with
his body beneath the cold assault. It was so easy to be
brave in the daylight, he thought, where he was warm
and safe and protected. It was a different thing to be
shivering in the dark, cold and alone, with only his
faith to protect him from his fears.

If he were running with the pack within this storm,
they would simply bury themselves beneath it, escaping
the freezing gale. But tonight there would be no escape.
Tonight there would be only the darkness, the shadows
that cloaked his doubts, and the howling wind that
slowly froze his body with ice and frost. And there
would be the heaviest burden to his tired soul: the
yearning for safety and family and the comfort of the
pack. Always his family had been his strength, and

although Gianavel had taught him to hunt and survive alone, Aramus had always leaned upon the old wolf's awesome strength.

As the chilling wind slowed and the snow fell heavily over him, the silver wolf's mind turned again to a warm, cozy den, his family at his side, and his father's soothing voice talking of the Lightmaker, the Old Story, and a glorious world awaiting. Even now, amidst the icy mist and deepening snow, Aramus felt his father's strength, so close. . . .

At a distance, Aramus much resembled his massive sire, although the older wolf held a distinct advantage in the balance of sheer weight and solidness of strength. But Aramus had inherited the promise of Gianavel's giant frame and symmetry, and already the young wolf's hard muscles rolled and swelled beneath his silver coat. Yet where his father's mane was deep gray from the long years, Aramus bore a mane of willowy silver. And where his father's gray eyes seemed to forever cloak wisdom and strength, Aramus still looked upon the world with shining silver eyes that always betrayed his thoughts, feelings, and fears.

For a moment Aramus thought of Lucas, his friend and companion, who would one day also endure the Watch. Only yesterday they had rested together, warm in the sun, on a rocky crag. They had sworn to always be together, friends forever, until death separated them, at last.

Lucas had been the first to speak of the ritual awaiting Aramus. His voice was thin, and the sun seemed subdued and shadowed as he spoke, though the sky was clear.

"I'm afraid," he said, as a bright red bird fluttered about his head. "They say that evil wolves live in the Deep Woods. And some of the Elders have suffered terrible battles there. If you go alone, as your father says you must, then something might happen to you. But I know what we can do. I can follow you. And we can go through the Watch together. No one will know. Then you will be safe."

Aramus had smiled sadly.

"No, my friend," he said. "I must go alone. My father has spoken. But he tells me that I can overcome the things I fear."

Lucas had fallen silent, and Aramus pondered his father's words.

"Sometimes . . . my father confuses me. He says there is nothing in the darkness that I should fear. But it is hard for me to believe that. I believe in the Lightmaker, but I don't know how to believe like my father. And sometimes when I ask him about it, he only says that my time hasn't come. He says that when the test of faith is upon me, the Lightmaker will give me the strength to endure. And then he talks a lot about living what I believe. I agree with him, and nod my head, but I really don't know what he's talking about."

Aramus paused, considering the words of the old wolf.

"He tells me that when I love the Lightmaker with all my heart, I'll find the secret of strength. But I'm not sure what he means. I already believe in the Lightmaker. And I'm still afraid."

Lucas remained silent, his white face reflecting the doubts that dwelled within. "I don't think that you'll survive the Watch," he said. "I had a dream last night that you were lost in a storm and something horrible was coming for you out of the dark. Its eyes burned with hate. Its fangs were wet with blood. And it was calling your name. But someone was with you, someone who loved you, who would protect you. I couldn't see who it was. I only know that he was strong and silent and close. Then the beast came, and there was a terrible battle, and death. I don't understand. I don't want you to go."

Aramus felt his mane bristle as he listened to Lucas describe his dream. For a moment his mind raced, searching for a meaning. But he knew he would find no answers. Finally, he leaned forward and nudged his friend.

"I don't understand, either," he said. "But I know that my father has spoken, and he's not going to tell me twice. It's my time for the Watch. But you and I will always be friends."

Lucas had gazed at him quietly, a mournful shadow casting his snow-white head.

"Friends forever," said Lucas.

Aramus nodded his head. "Friends forever."

And then night had cast long shadows, and the young wolves had returned to their dens. But Aramus did not sleep through the long night, anxiously awaiting the journey that would begin with day.

Early, before the sun crested the horizon, he had begun the long run south with his father. As they loped easily toward the first high ridge that marked their mountain home, Aramus had felt eyes on his back. At the top of the ridge he hesitated, glancing behind, and saw Lucas gazing mournfully at him from atop a small hill. Aramus had raised his head, signaling that he would return with the morning. And Lucas had raised his head also, but with the gesture came a low and lonely cry that beckoned to Aramus across the distance, and carried through the forest at his back.

His friend's last cry had echoed in Aramus's mind every step of the journey, and Gianavel had seemed subdued and quiet, as if dreading the task at hand. Finally, at sunset, they had arrived at the border of the Deep Woods, where his father had led him to a wide glade. Then the great gray wolf had turned toward the trail that ran north, leaving him alone for the long night's ritual.

At the place where the trail disappeared into the forest, Gianavel hesitated, looking back. The mists of twilight swirled past the august head, and in that fleeting, transparent moment, Aramus sensed something hidden within his father's gray eyes, almost as if the old wolf were cloaking some sacred secret. The farewell that Aramus had heard so many times was all but lost in the wind, but he knew the words in his heart.

"Be strong. Be courageous. Do what you know is right," the old voice spoke against the night.

Then, in a ghostly, silent turn, he was gone in the gray mist. . . .

The hours had passed slowly since his sire had vanished in the mist that had settled into a storm. Aramus shivered beneath his silver coat and blinked against the icy wind that howled across the glade. The storm was gathering strength.

Suddenly Aramus caught an alien scent on the night wind. Instinctively he raised his head, and ice shattered on his silver mane as he lifted his nose to know the faint scent borne on the freezing gale. Fully alert, he searched the wind, the shadows, the air, to find the intruder's location. But as quickly as the scent had come, it was gone again, the icy wind shifting to rush at him from across the wide, white glade in a waving wall of sleet.

Shivering, Aramus remained poised, sensing the darkness mocking him. And he gazed restlessly into the night.

"Be strong," he repeated numbly, hearing the words from a distance. "That's what he said. Do what you know is right. Strength . . . will come."

But it seemed so far beyond him now; his faith so small, his fear so great. He did believe. But he did not know how to find strength in what he believed.

A savage gale smashed ice across his silver head. Aramus winced, bending forward as the wind brought him to the coldest, cruelest cell of the storm. Struggling, he lifted his head, searching the sky with pleading eyes, but saw only desolation, darkness. He lowered his head wearily, sensing a devastating loneliness, as if whatever battle to be fought, whatever life he might have found . . . was already lost.

"Alone . . ." he whispered. "I'm alone. . . ."

e i g h t

Suddenly a faint sound that did not carry with the hushed, swaying branches caught Aramus's attention. Even above the rushing wind he sensed shuffling movements to the south. And in the space of a single breath his entire body was poised, focusing on the whisper beneath the storm. With eyes keen to the dim light he searched the darkness, prepared to fight with a split second's warning. Instinctively his lips drew back, revealing two long canines that distended to his lower jaw, the warning that preceded combat. Yet he made no sound to reveal his presence, as he had been taught.

Almost instantly Aramus realized that the intruder was moving straight toward him, and would be upon him in an instant. He heard every step, every muffled footfall, every limb that bent before its motion, and his mane bristled as he anticipated some dark and terrible creature that fed upon the night.

Then in a frantic rustling the movement hastened, the sound of something rushing through the night to his place of hiding. With quivering muscles Aramus followed each quick step as the intruder burst across the last remaining space between them. Then the dark figure hurtled out of the brush, only a small space away.

Aramus was a spinning silver wheel as he exploded from the snow, his roar shattering the night. Bounding blindingly to the side, he lashed out with a long foreleg to strike the intruder to the ground. But even as his foreleg flashed white in the starlight, the wolf recognized the small figure for what it was. And before his powerful blow would have crushed the life from its form, he turned the impact aside to send the intruder tumbling harmlessly into the snow, and effortlessly pinned it with a wide paw.

For at the last deadly moment Aramus had realized that the furry figure was not a creature feared by his kind. Rather, it was one of the fun-loving, peaceful creatures who lived beneath the hills and dales far to the south.

Aramus almost smiled as he pinned it to the ground, but even as he touched its wet chest, his nose caught the scent of blood on the night air and he knew that something was strangely, horribly wrong.

The smell of fresh wounds filled the night. And in the moment of silence that followed the confrontation, Aramus saw terrible slashes in the hare's chest and legs.

A mangling wound lay across its shoulder and foreleg, and one side of its furry face was matted black. One ear was ripped and bleeding, as if from thorns. And as the long moments passed, Aramus began to make out other, more serious wounds hidden beneath the matted blood.

Aramus did not know much about the hare's kind, but he had seen death enough in his life. Even though the creature still had the strength to run haltingly through the forest night, he knew its wounds were mortal.

For a long time he held it to the snow and studied its form more carefully. Slowly he realized, with a growing dread, that its injuries were the slash marks of a gigantic wolf. But the hare was strong and old in years, and did not die easily. Its face was drawn with pain, and it breathed haltingly, clinging to life with desperate strength.

The moments crept by in silence, and Aramus felt the small body growing cold beneath him. Remarkably, the hare seemed to be resting, never resisting his solid hold nor attempting to struggle away from the force that imprisoned him. Aramus had begun to think that it would never open its dark eyes when finally the soft brown lids parted, revealing shades of deeper brown staring back at him.

The hare did not appear afraid of the huge snout that hovered inches away. Rather, there was a sad, quiet resignation. Almost, it seemed, as if the small creature had abandoned hope of escaping whatever he had fled so frantically through the forest night.

In his curiosity Aramus forgot the night, the Deep
Woods, and the Watch. For here was a small creature,
caught in his grasp, gravely wounded yet running with
its last strength through these cursed woods. And he
felt something strange in the air about it, something
terrible, and monstrous; something he had felt only once
before. Something so hideous that the arctic air seemed
to grow warm with its hate.

A long moment passed, both creatures breathing in
silence. In another time, another place, the hare would
have been food for Aramus. But not here, and not now.
For this small creature feared something beyond them
both. Something that might even now be chasing it
through the winter night to this lonely place.

Finally, when Aramus could wait no longer, he spoke.
"I will not harm you," he said.

The hare did not appear startled at his words. His
eyes focused intently on Aramus, and for a long moment
he did not reply. Aramus solemnly studied the creature
in the frosty light, while the storm raged over his
shoulders, swirling snow across their heads.

Then a small voice whispered to him in the misty air.

"No," the hare said quietly, and sighed. "You will
not . . . harm me . . . this night."

Aramus forced himself to wait patiently as the
creature recovered from his long effort. It was clear the
hare had run far, driven by some final force of will.
After a time the wounded creature managed to speak
again, marshalling whatever strength still remained in its
dying flesh.

"It is an evil far stronger than us both . . . that hunts me through the night. An evil you should flee. For it will destroy you . . . as well . . . when it comes."

A long pause followed, with the hare drawing deep breaths, eyes closed. He was relaxed now, Aramus sensed. Whatever desperate strength had driven it on and on through the endless night was drained, depleted. Age and those deadly wounds had taken their final toll.

And as the wolf watched, the old hare opened his eyes again, and spoke softly. "I think I shall rest here . . . for a while. I have run far enough. And I am growing cold . . . with morning so close."

Aramus felt the hare's deep wounds quiver with his words. He removed his foreleg, shielding the small form as best he could beneath his thickly coated chest, protecting it from the merciless wind that slashed them with sleet and snow. Silently, he studied the hare's condition, wondering how long it would last before death followed those massive wounds.

"What has done this to you?" he said quietly.

The hare breathed heavily, once, his chin resting upon his chest, then fell very still. For a long moment Aramus was afraid that he had died. Then the hare raised his head, as if fighting off sleep, and spoke.

"There is no time. I know . . . that you are here . . . for a purpose. I have heard of the gray wolves, and I know that they, too, worship the Lightmaker. But you must flee this place. A great beast is coming. He will kill you, too. So . . . leave quickly. Or there will be no escape."

The hare breathed slowly, quietly, then stiffened, as if to escape some unendurable agony, before relaxing once again.

"Little time remains. I fear that already . . . too many have died. It lives only to destroy those who worship the Lightmaker."

Aramus knew.

"Baalkor," he whispered

The old hare looked into his eyes. "That is . . . its name? . . . Yes, so it seems."

Wounded breathing rasped in the night air.

"I have led it far from my home, deep into these cursed woods. And Windgate led my colony . . . his colony . . . south to the caves beside the brook. There, they will be safe. And now you must not stay. I sense your faith, and I know that you, too, worship the Lightmaker. But there is no cause for more sacrifice. To stay . . . is doom."

Aramus saw tears form in the tired eyes.

"So much love, yet we were too weak. I heard the cries of the little ones. And I did not see poor Benjamin rise. But for brave Windgate, we all would have been destroyed. It has no mercy. I have never . . . seen its equal. You are young, and strong, but it is twice your strength, and more. Save yourself."

The hare's words ended with a quiet sigh, and he lowered his head again upon his chest. His eyes were closed and swollen from his mourning, and his breath became shallow and cold.

Sorrow touched Aramus to know that this small creature had endured such terror. Yet he was also seized by dread to discover that Baalkor, the dark beast who had killed Karidural and fought his father in the frozen North, was stalking through the forest night, hunting this hare to finish a fight that should never have begun.

Suddenly, a demonic howl hurled from some distant, darkened ridge invaded the night sky. And Aramus stood, startled, recognizing instantly a cry he had never heard. His breath caught in his chest, and if it were possible he would have looked across the endless night to behold the beast. But he could not. He looked again to the hare, his silver eyes searching.

The small creature gazed back at him, old and prepared.

"Yes," he said, nodding. "It is coming."

Such death for the sake of death alone made Aramus's mane bristle. And in his mind he could see Baalkor, that ancient destroyer of lives, rushing silently through the night to this lonely place, fangs fresh with the blood of the innocent, dark eyes burning with hate.

In horror, the frightened wolf remembered Lucas's dream: the dream of Death rising from its hellish grave, whispering his name.

nine

Aramus studied the haggard moon that hung oppressively above the distant ridge. Everything he knew told him to flee this evil place. There was nothing he could do for the hare. And to stay would mean death. But still he hesitated, his heart touched, his spirit compelled to reach out, embracing the wounded creature.

He laid down again beside the old hare.

Aramus knew that soon the sun would rise and burn away the storm, but the last of the night remained. He shook his head, sensing defeat. He had almost made it to the morning, hidden silently within the snow. And now he was faced with a deadly confrontation that he had done his best to avoid. The dawn seemed too far away as he searched the mist for the horror he feared approaching. He looked again upon the hare.

Ice slowly formed across the wolf's back as he protected the small creature, but the cold was forgotten as Aramus wrestled with the terrible decision of whether to abandon his post and suffer defeat in the Watch, or remain and face the beast that might come upon them before dawn.

Aramus knew that his father would never leave the Watch; not for fear of the storm, or the cold, or any beast that lived. Countless times Aramus had seen Gianavel stand in the gap, defending the pack against lion or bear. Often the battles had been fierce beyond endurance, but the great wolf had never retreated, had never fallen beneath the terrible onslaught. And in the end, he had always prevailed; wounded and scarred, but saving the lives of those who needed him. Aramus had learned much from his sire, for his father was one who lived as he spoke.

Thinking of his father's size and strength, Aramus studied the old hare's quiet form, wondering how the small creature could even begin to resist Baalkor.

"I have met this thing before," said Aramus. "Not long ago I saw something in the dark. I wanted to run. But I was too scared. Then my father came and rescued me. And if he hadn't, I would have died. How can you be so brave when you know that it's coming for you?"

The hare smiled weakly, his tired face settling in familiar lines. He seemed stronger now, recovering slowly beneath the warmth of Aramus's silver coat, sharing the heat of the wolf's massive form.

"Flesh is flesh," he said. "I'm afraid, too, sometimes.
It is the way of things. But as you grow older, strength
comes, little by little. Endurance is gained by enduring.
My strength has become greater with each struggle I
have faced in my long, long life."

Then the hare began to speak again, and ceased. His
old eyes looked into the forest, or the night, or something beyond them both. And for a long moment he
focused on the dark. Then his eyes seemed to laugh,
though Aramus could not be sure.

"So much love . . . yet you do not know," he said,
nodding lightly. "It would be a great honor, one day,
perhaps in a world beyond this, to know your father. He
is one who loves much, and lives his love."

Suddenly the hare stiffened, brown eyes shut tightly,
and the old, scarred face was a reflection of agony as he
suffered from some abysmal, mortal pain.

Aramus waited, watching sadly.

Again a demonic howl split the sky, closer than
before. Aramus lifted his head and listened. The dark
sound was moving, even as it haunted the night. The
beast was coming faster now, no longer confused by the
hare's final tricks to evade its pursuit. Aramus listened
nervously until the victorious voice vanished from the
mist, dreading that it would be upon them all too soon.
Then he turned his attention to the hare.

The warm brown eyes were closed, and beneath the
blood that masked its wounds, Aramus could not discern
whether he still breathed. Then the hare weakly raised
his head, and spoke with a ghostly stare.

"Leave quickly. The greater danger . . . is yours. It will destroy you, too, at the last. But he will not kill you outright. He will want to destroy your spirit and leave your flesh alive, if he can. That is the greater victory. He will frighten you, and tempt you with dark pleasures, hoping you will prefer evil desires over suffering for what is right. If you stay, you must not listen to him. He is too strong for you. Choose whom you will serve by faith. That is all you need to know. It is the final stand, and Baalkor cannot overcome it. But beware. When he fails to turn you from your faith, he will try to destroy you, as he has with me. But I was prepared . . . to die. And now that my fight is finished, I am content. I have endured . . . to the end."

Aramus saw that a peace beyond this life had already touched the hare's heart, and he searched for words to ease the small creature's pain, but nothing seemed enough.

"What is your name?" he asked softly.

The hare breathed once, deeply.

"I am Saul," he said.

A malignant mist thickened on the far side of the glade. Aramus watched it roll toward them, swept by the relentless, freezing winds, and he struggled for words that might give them hope.

"There's still a chance that you'll live," he said. "Maybe my father will return. He's not afraid of any-thing. The dark wolf will never attack us if he is here." Aramus paused, ashamed. "But I've always failed to defeat my fears. And I'll probably fail you, too."

Saul smiled, and for the first time seemed to laugh in the wolf's embrace. "I do not fail . . . when my heart is true," he said quietly. "Nor shall you."

Silver eyes gazed tenderly, softly, upon the hare.

"You only think you're going to fail because you have always failed," Saul whispered. "I was much the same when I was your age. You try to overcome your weakness, your fears, with the strength of your flesh. But it is the strength of the spirit that enables you to overcome. It is not something you can understand with your mind. It's something you must know in your heart. This is the mystery that defeats the world."

Weighed down by his great, ponderous fatigue and an emptiness that reached into desolation, Aramus stirred his strength.

"How do I know this strength?" he asked. "My father talks like you do. But I only feel alone, as I felt tonight. Though sometimes, when I'm hurt, I think I might feel something . . . in my heart. I'm not sure. Is that when the Lightmaker comes to us, when we're hurt?"

"The Lightmaker is always with you," Saul said gently. "But our hearts are filled with many things, so we don't hear him. That's why so often it's only in times of suffering that we finally understand, because it is then we finally listen. And then we come to know his love for us. We become one with the Lightmaker, and strength comes for the task.

"Don't feel that you are alone. Everyone must endure . . . the Dark Night of the Soul. Sometimes it lasts for days. Sometimes it lasts for years. But it is something we must all endure, to find our strength. There is no shame in your pain. It only means that the Lightmaker is working within you, burning away everything that makes you weak. Don't run from the pain. Embrace it bravely, and look into your heart. Then allow the Lightmaker to destroy within you all those things that keep you from him. The pain is great, but in the end, if you will only endure, you will stand in new strength, and a new life."

With Saul's words, Aramus felt both his fears and his courage blazing more brightly than ever before. For he was looking upon death, a slow, painful death. Yet he was seeing something more. He was seeing life and courage, of a kind the young wolf had never witnessed before, not even in the great gray Elders of his pack. They were brave in battle and strong in the winter, but this small one was their equal in courage, perhaps even greater. Here was one who held strength beyond fang and claw. In a strange, uncanny way, Aramus felt his heart draw closer to Saul, a creature he could call . . . friend.

As Saul spoke, snow had drifted into a crusted mound about Aramus's side. And although he had protected the small creature from the storm, Aramus knew that there was a greater danger coming out of the mist, a danger he could not defeat.

A booming howl, terrifyingly close, shattered the night air and swept across the glade. The howl ended harshly, terminating in a series of beastly barks. Unblinking, Aramus looked toward the sound, determining its distance, though in the mist and storm he could not be sure. And as his penetrating stare fixed on the far side of the frozen glade, a light flashed behind his silver eyes. Then he turned back, without expression, to his friend.

Saul was resting. His breathing had tired, and his shaking slowed. Aramus saw that his companion's strength was fading, for perhaps the final time. The old voice was thin and weak when the hare spoke again.

"His grace is sufficient . . . his grace is sufficient . . . always strength comes . . . for the task."

Saul's words echoed in the early morning air long after he had ceased to speak. The moon was ragged and pale where it glared between patches of cloud. A cold wind moaned across the glade, and white mist rolled over them. Aramus lifted up his head and sensed something very close, barely beyond the storm. His fears, the old nature, the urge to flee, struggled vainly to rise within him, and he smiled faintly, grimly, at the thought. He knew what he would do.

"I'll never leave you," Aramus said, looking softly upon his dying friend. "We are servants of the Light-maker. We will live together, or die together. And if we are still alive when morning comes, I'll carry you back home to your family. Even if you . . . die . . . I'll carry you home. I promise."

Saul seemed to smile.

"A promise made, a promise kept, when love would mean so much. Strength may fail, the eye grow dim . . . but the heart shall ever last."

Saul began to speak again and ceased, and a touch of sadness was in his eyes as he rolled his head weakly to the side, gazing into the mist. And Aramus knew that Saul sensed what could not be heard, coming out of the night.

"... the beast is here," he said.

t e n

Aramus sensed the deadly chill that brushed across his back and was already rising at the old hare's words. Instinctively the mane bristled along his spine and his fangs emerged in a ghastly white snarl. A promise made, now left to keep, he turned to face the beast.

The mist thickened, as if hiding something hideous that whispered to them from beyond the pale shroud. Then slowly, hauntingly, a shape seemed to reveal itself, emerging from the storm as if it were taking substance from the night. Darkness appeared to fall before it as the beast came out of the mist. It separated from the night, a malignant shadow coming out of the storm, and left no footprints as it crossed the snow.

Its dead eyes marked its soul, born in the night and wed with the grave. Glowing darkly, they fixed on the hare, and for a long moment Aramus stood spellbound

at the wolf's size. Even larger than Gianavel, it moved
with the grace of a lion. And its dark head stood against
a colossal mound of scarred flesh, marked with the
wounds of terrible battles. Its body seemed to still be
emerging from the mist long after its head and
monstrous forelimbs had come into the moonlight. Then
finally it was there, huge and godlike with red fangs
glistening in distended jaws. In his fear Aramus saw it as
some lost lord of the underworld, set loose from its
hellish throne to stalk the Earth in the power of Night.

If Aramus had not moved, the beast would have
passed him without notice, intent on the hare who had
earlier escaped his wrath. Then, as he had seen his
father do so many times against lion and bear, Aramus
threw himself in the gap and unleashed a deafening roar.

Baalkor halted suddenly, seeming to notice the silver
wolf for the first time. The scent of fresh blood reached
Aramus, and he saw the red jaws and blackened claws.
Eyes like dried blood turned toward him, and he felt his
skin shiver at the sight. Beneath that unearthly stare
Aramus felt his snarl fade and his strength fall, his
courage crushed by its demonic will.

The monster's gaze measured Aramus, and instinctively the young wolf took firmer footing in the thickly
crusted snow, tensing for the first deadly lunge. Behind
him he heard Saul shuffling weakly on the snowy
mound.

Baalkor seemed to study him, a mocking smile curling
cruel black lips. Aramus prayed for strength equal to the
task.

And finally, as if the challenge had lost all cause for amusement, the monster spoke.

"So, you will defend the poor, pitiful creature?"

Aramus said nothing. The battle was already beyond words.

"How very noble. I am sure that when your father returns to find your dead body in the glade, he will know that you died well."

It smiled. Inside the dark eyes a ghostly red haze shivered menacingly.

"You serve the Lightmaker," it intoned. "I serve the Dark Lord. Give me the hare or die."

Its hate filled the arctic night, and the trees seemed to shrink from its presence as it spoke. The stars, already weak and dry, paled at its words. The wind fell eerily still.

Dread crawled through Aramus as he stared into the icy depths of the black eyes, and feared the darkness that dwelled within.

Then, faintly, words left to him with the dying sun returned, echoing dimly along the shadowed corridors of his shattered spirit.

"Be strong. Be courageous. Do what you know is right."

Aramus drew upon his staggering courage.

"I am Aramus, son of Gianavel. I am a servant of the Lightmaker, as my father before me. I stand against you."

Baalkor's eyes gleamed hungrily.

"Gianavel . . . my enemy," it drew the words out deliciously, "my great, hated enemy! This will be a delicacy indeed. Vengeance fulfilled twice in a night! A dead king and the son of a king. There will be no one left to slay."

Baalkor threw back its head, laughing soundlessly, fangs gleaming. Aramus thrilled with a new surge of fear that made his legs tremble despite his resolve.

Dark eyes turned on him again.

"Don't you know me, boy?" it rasped. The beast appeared to grow distant from Aramus, as if separated by a deeper, descending darkness that held the power to delay the dawn.

Aramus stared, eyes wide.

"You are Baalkor," he said, finally. "You are an old wolf, one of the Dark Council."

A silent, laughing rage made Baalkor seem even more monstrous. Within its eyes, dark flames danced into endless night.

"Oh, I am much more than an old wolf, boy. Much more. The darkness that holds you is my child. The grave that will claim you is my bride. The horror you feel in your heart is my love. There is no power that can defeat me. I am a servant of the Dark Lord, the end of the Earth. I live only to slay the living. And the hills hold the bones to mark my passing. I am the beast you fear in the night. I am the thing that waits for you in the dark. I am hunger. I am pain. I am Death."

The cold wind moaned silently behind its words, and Aramus felt his legs grow weak. A wild, overpowering fear made him tense as if to run, but he stilled himself, holding his ground in a stance without strength. Then

he heard Saul shuffling behind him, and his courage
endured. Unconsciously Aramus braced himself for a
firmer grip in the snow before he spoke.

"You can't have him."

Baalkor shifted slightly in the snow. Its black tongue
flicked across the fangs mockingly.

"Can't you see how the Lightmaker has forsaken the
hare?" it said, its voice suddenly soothing, calmer. "Do
you not see his terrible wounds? If the Lightmaker were
truly alive do you believe that Saul would be wounded
unto death? No. The Lightmaker would fight to defend
you. That is a sign that the Lightmaker is gone. The
days of Saul's faith have ended, as they were meant to
end. Come, let us reason together. Clearly, the Lightmaker is not here. It is only the three of us. I admire
you, young cub. You are brave to face me to defend this
creature. But your sacrifice is foolish. What has the
Lightmaker done for you? You are alone in the cold
dark, facing certain death. And look at Saul. He is dead
already. I don't even have to finish the task. That is
what the Lightmaker does for you. He forsakes you
when you need him the most."

Baalkor bent its dark head forward.

"Join me," it whispered, fangs rasping, "let us feast on
the hare as brothers. Join me, and you will never look
upon suffering again. All the pleasures of the world will
be yours. Nothing will be withheld from your sight. Join
me, and the Dark Lord will fulfill all your secret desires,
the pleasures you have every right to enjoy. Only forget
the Old Story. The Lightmaker is a dream, a dream of

fools. And the Age of Dreams has ended. We are the New Creation, the purpose of all things, the beginning of all things. Pleasure and power are our dreams, dreams we now fulfill. Forget this useless faith, this foolish suffering, and accept the unending pleasures the Dark Lord can give you."

Aramus stared, shaken, even as a shadowy haze descended within his mind, an otherworldly darkness that dimmed his reason and sought a stronghold in his heart.

Even as Baalkor continued his soothing speech.

"For behold the power of the Dark Lord. I am greater among wolves than any living. And yet I am not alone; legion stand behind me. Many are the dark wolves who have come across to the greater power of Night. We take the Earth, destroying what we wish. Nothing can stop us. Yet I am least of the Dark Council. I will not fail to speak of Incomel, the great lion who destroys at will and stands above me in rank. Alone, he is equal to your entire pack in strength. Strike at him once, and it will be your doom. He sees in the night as in the day, and is feared even by servants of darkness. And yet he is but a shadow of Corbis, the great bear who is our chief. Corbis, god on the Earth, second only to the Dark Lord in the strength and power of his wrath. Corbis, who makes the Earth tremble when he walks and breaks trees like rotten straw. Sorrow covers the land when he rises up in his wrath, and the sight of him casts down all hope for life. What good is it to stand against us? Those who are with me are greater than those who are with

you. How could we hold such power if the Dark Lord
were not supreme?"

Aramus felt as if unseen claws had sliced painful
wounds through his spirit. He shook his head, throwing
off snow and shadows together, struggling to resist the
overpowering force of the beast. But its power was
beyond flesh, the spell hypnotic, making him weary
unto death with the effort of resisting its enduring
strength.

Baalkor's black head bent conspiratorially.

"Join me, and greater power awaits us, still. We will
change this land. Only we must first free the world of
these creatures who have corrupted it with their infernal, twisted faith. Then the world will be pure and we
will receive the true power of the Dark Lord. We will
pass beyond flesh, beyond knowledge, beyond strength.
We will know the ancient secrets, hold the keys of
eternal life and death. And when the last of this
creature's kind are finally wiped from the earth, the
Dark Lord will deliver us, making us what we were truly
meant to be: gods."

Baalkor commanded the night, and spoke without
fear.

"Join me."

Aramus tried to focus on the dark beast before him,
but saw as one sees in a dream. His mind was worn,
torn down and ravaged by the power of its irresistible
will. There were so many things he did not know, so
many things he did not understand. Was there any truth
in Baalkor's words? Truly, where was the Lightmaker in

this dark hour? And what would happen should death take him? Saddened, confused, he turned helplessly toward his wounded friend for some answer, some hope, to the doubts that struck him down.

Saul only gazed at him with strong, loving eyes, and the ghost of a smile seemed to touch the tiny mouth as he spoke.

"Choose this day . . . whom you will serve," was all he said.

Aramus blinked, then slowly smiled back at his friend. The silver wolf's heart swelled with tenderness. Remembering, now, that he had already known it would come to this. For long ago Gianavel had taught him that in this world he must forever choose who he would serve. He would serve the Lightmaker, or he would serve the Dark Lord. For there was nothing else. Always there would be mysteries, questions that he could not answer. But on this day, in this hour, he could choose who he would serve . . . by faith.

His choice made, the path was clear.

Silver eyes turned to his enemy.

"Words of a dying fool!" growled Baalkor, blasting frost from his jaws in an evil cloud. "Will you listen to one who is at death's door? I am stronger. The Dark Lord is greater than your worthless Lightmaker. I have beaten you."

Aramus lowered his hard shoulders before he spoke. "No."

For a long moment Baalkor pondered the response, a hideous haze shadowing its head.

Then slowly, from somewhere within, it seemed to summon an awesome and terrible power, as if it were calling the Dark Lord himself forth from some nightmarish throne of darkness. A snarl that began deep in the dark wolf's chest trembled the snow and ground beneath it. And the black head lowered, whispering the names of fallen foes. Then in a nightmare it moved, exploding in a devastating rush. Almost instantly the black and red avalanche was upon Aramus, who was unprepared for such a blinding attack. Gaping fangs reached his throat, and a paralyzing roar froze his heart.

eleven

E ven as the dark form descended upon him, Aramus moved, spinning sideways to narrowly evade the monstrous force that crushed the ground where he had stood. Only at the last moment did Baalkor's fangs follow, leaving a deep searing wound along his ribs.

Instantly its huge paw lashed out, striking him forcefully across the face. Yet in his fury Aramus did not feel the pain, only a rage that flamed within him, a rage to turn and destroy this evil beast that had come against them.

And as Aramus frantically struggled to regain his balance, Baalkor suddenly threw its great weight full against him, colliding with terrific force. Aramus was stunned. The painful impact blasted the breath from his lungs and sent him sprawling onto his back, dazed and disoriented. And then the beast was above him, jaws ready to descend, a gaping maw of ragged swords that could sever his head from his neck.

With strength born of desperation, Aramus brought his hind legs up, raking savagely to disembowel his evil foe. And they found the soft underbelly of the beast, tearing furiously.

In rage and pain Baalkor turned to the side, seeking to escape the young wolf's tearing claws. For one fleeting second the weight above Aramus lifted, and with a tactic he had long used in play against his brothers, he twisted violently, dislodging his foe. Then in a quick spin he regained his stance, retreating with a roar.

Enraged, Aramus dimly recognized the taste of blood on his fangs, and he knew that, somehow, he had also struck in the deadly encounter. But his leg almost collapsed beneath him as he retreated, surprising him with the depth of his wound. And he frantically tensed his muscles, willing the leg to regain strength.

Baalkor seemed to gloat in its unavoidable victory. It was master here, it knew, and in a moment it would crush the life out of this thing, this servant of the Lightmaker who stood between him and the world.

Aramus circled back, seeking an opening, but Baalkor advanced with unnerving calm. It seemed to savor the moment, as if its victory were already complete. A mocking smile touched the black lips, curling them to reveal glistening jaws tinged with his blood. Aramus remembered the horrible face poised in the night.

And then, with a thrill of panic, he realized that he was about to die. He was going to die out here in this frozen glade. All those long hours his father had spent teaching him to survive seemed so useless now. He had sensed Baalkor's irresistible strength when it collided against him. It was like black granite, carved from the walls of Hell itself, driven by supernatural rage. Aramus realized that the beast was only toying with him, not even touching the true power hidden within its massive form.

Baalkor advanced slowly, grinning, doom clouding its head.

Aramus had retreated almost to Saul, roaring and using false attacks to stall the dark wolf. But the monster moved forward, implacable, undisturbed by any threat.

Aramus felt the ground steepening behind him, marking the beginning of the true forest edge where the trail ran north to his home. His footing quickly became uncertain in the deeper snow that covered the layers of dead leaves and limbs. Then, without warning, his hind leg slid though a tangle of limbs hidden by the snow. Aramus frantically tore his leg free, anticipating an attack during the quick distraction. But Baalkor only seemed to laugh, moving slowly forward. And Aramus knew he could retreat no further.

Aramus felt a movement near him on the hillside, and with a frantic glance he saw that Saul was struggling to his feet, dying yet determined to defy, prepared to fight beside him against this demonic beast of unspeakable power and rage . . . and suddenly, he knew.

In that quick and terrible moment when hideous Death rose before him, and his wounded friend struggled to rise beside him, Aramus knew, and understood, the secret of strength; understanding that the world had no power over Saul because there was nothing left of the world within him. Saul was free, and the freedom was power: the power to choose what was right, the power to resist the darkness, and the power to die without fear because his life was with the Lightmaker, a life that could never be taken from him, not by suffering, or danger, or death.

And in that instant, as Aramus felt and understood the secret, he overcame the world, choosing to love the Lightmaker with all his heart and soul, sensing spirit and love that flowed into strength, giving him the power to resist, lifting his life beyond reach of the beast.

Aramus's screaming snarl snatched the dark wolf's attention for a long chilling instant. And a pale flicker flashed behind the black eyes as the silver wolf advanced.

"I know what you are, beast," he said. "You are a liar, and a coward. It is you who should fear death. For you will die once, and then suffer judgment. But we will survive the night because we do not belong to the world. So fight me, if you dare. Death cannot claim me."

Aramus roared savagely and threw himself forward, gaining momentum in the last quick surge to collide against Baalkor with all his weight. And the dark wolf slid back at the impact, its legs skidding out on the snow. Yet with the painful collision Aramus felt as if he had thrown himself against a mountain wall. The bruising concussion sent him sprawling to the side, and in the next chaotic moment a long foreleg lashed out, striking him across the eyes.

Light flashed across his mind, and Aramus felt the ground swing away beneath him. For a long white moment he tumbled through space, a demonic laugh roaring through his mind. Then he crashed heavily in the snow. A frenzied movement followed, with Baalkor crushing him, and as blood streaked his silver mane Aramus knew that he was wounded again.

Baalkor's dark face glowered over him, red jaws glistening with hell within, and flashed toward his face. But as the black wedge descended, Aramus twisted to the side and his own sharp fangs found their mark. The dark wolf howled, twisted back, and broke clear of the grip. Then it surged forward again.

Aramus struggled to regain his footing, but the monster struck him full force. He was hurled back, searching for ground, and crashed heavily into a cold tangle of icy limbs. It was the remnant of a giant oak that had fallen years before, yet which still held thick branches imprisoning him on all sides. Roaring, Aramus savagely tore against the clinging branches, shattering ice and limbs alike, knowing Baalkor would use the moment to kill Saul.

And even as Aramus raged against the icy prison, he saw the dark wolf moving toward Saul, its frosty breath streaming in clouds.

Baalkor's words were venom.

"I have defeated you. The Dark Lord is greater."

Saul seemed to look with quiet separation at the great black beast. Already, Aramus thought, his mind and spirit are in another place, somehow unreachable by the monster that loomed over him. But there was no time left to think. Aramus twisted violently and felt a limb break across his back. Several quick, tearing motions began to shake him free.

And strangely, above it all, he heard Saul's quiet response.

"And tell me, Death, where is your power... to hold me in the grave?"

Baalkor's breath vanished in the night air, and its face seemed to blacken with the thought. For a long moment it was frozen in the faint light of the approaching dawn, the dark forehead reflecting the madness that raced across its mind. An abomination thickened about it, as if an ancient and hideous hate settled on its brow. Even the night seemed to retreat from its anger, while Saul remained unbent, and unafraid. Then with all his strength Aramus tore free, leaping forward.

Baalkor also moved, with a roar of madness and rage. It launched itself into the air toward Saul, dark flames sailing before it, with the great black form itself deeper than the night.

They met in the air over the hare, two titanic shapes reared against the stars, fangs flashing in the growing light, who struck together and crashed like thunder to the earth.

They descended in a deadly embrace, roaring and striking in a blinding exchange of fang and claw. And as they smashed into the ice, they revolved across the frozen glade, swirling in a thunderstorm of blows, leaving scarlet ribbons in the snow.

With unbelievable strength Baalkor grasped Aramus's silver mane between knifelike canines and shook with all his weight. Aramus wrestled backwards against the assault, falling beneath the great crushing force and killing grip. Then, in a swift movement, he twisted to the side, in agony tearing his neck free from the fangs. But there was no retreat. Roaring, the young wolf hurled himself forward again, colliding against the beast's chest with all his massive strength.

For one fleeting instant Baalkor reeled back, off balance. And seizing the opening, Aramus leaped and closed upon a long foreleg. With desperate shakes he threw himself back. Beneath his fangs he felt the bone crack, and the dark wolf howled, slashing his face to break his grip.

Baalkor screamed and shook, hideous, scattering blood from a dozen wounds. Then in hellish rage it charged again, shattering crusted snow with a demonic roar. Aramus also charged, roaring in rage, and they collided like lions in the glade.

For a long moment they stood suspended on hind legs, two servants of two masters, resisting the other to the death. In a whirlwind of motion the dark wolf threw Aramus to the ground. Its flashing red maw descended, but slower, and fatigued. And as the dark head fell, Aramus caught it between powerful forelegs and his own jaws found its neck. Then he twisted, throwing the beast onto its back. The glade trembled as Baalkor crashed to the earth, and the silver wolf's fangs fell like lightning.

Howling, shaking blood from a great wound, Baalkor broke violently away, retreating with shaken snarls. Aramus started after it, as if to press the attack, then stopped. His silver mane was torn and streaked with crimson, but he felt no pain. He knew he had the strength to fight forever.

The dark wolf stood a distance apart, panting and livid, its face void of pride or glory. Fear behind pain gave a shallow depth to its eyes.

For a long moment they faced each other, breathing heavily, blood staining the ice beneath their feet. And then slowly, painfully, the shadow of defeat fell across Baalkor's scarred head, and Aramus heard its rasping voice for the final time.

"I will return."

Aramus did not move.

"I will be waiting," he said. "Always I stand between you and the world."

As the glade turned a deeper gold, and the sun's slanting rays threw the first thin shadows from the trees, the evil one turned and limped across the glade. Soon it had vanished in the mist.

Aramus knew in that moment that he had survived the night and the Watch. And sensing sadly what he would find, he turned back to his fallen friend.

Yet even as he whirled toward the forest edge he saw a massive shape glittering within the shadow of a giant oak, the shape of a silent and great gray wolf. Snow was crusted at his feet and lay in a heavy shroud across his shoulders, and he stood majestic and great and golden in the glowing dawn. Then Aramus understood the secret that his father had hidden from him at dusk. And he knew that the old wolf had never left him alone through the long winter night, but had watched over him through it all. The gray eyes gazed with wisdom and love from the thin gloom, and suddenly the cold was not so cold anymore.

Quietly Aramus returned to his friend. Saul was resting on the snowy hillside, and had watched wide-eyed the last great encounter. Aramus saw that his face was tired and peaceful, and he no longer shivered from the cold. Eternity had wrapped itself in a cloak about him, and his old eyes blinked slowly in the golden light. The moment had come, at last.

As farewell, the wolf leaned down, touching nose to nose with his friend. Saul closed his eyes and sighed.

"Your heart has stood the test," he said. "Always strength comes with the task. You found your life by living... what you knew... was true."

Then the hare grew still and raised his head. The
wolf watched in silence and awe.

"So much love, yet you never knew, he was with you
all the night." Then he lowered his head, and was quiet.

A cold wind moaned in the golden dawn and the
wounded wolf bowed his head. His friend was gone, the
battle won, leaving a last cherished promise to keep.

His father was beside him, the noble head lowered.
His mane was coated in ice, even now melting in the
dawn, but he seemed untouched by the cold, the great
shoulders strong and enduring, beyond the world's power
to destroy.

"You were with me through the night," said Aramus,
"and yet I never knew."

His father's presence was close about him in the
growing warmth of day. "I was with you through the
night, it's true," Gianavel said. "But it was not just of
me that he spoke."

Aramus glanced toward the place where Baalkor had
vanished into the thinning mist, but his heart lay beside
his fallen friend.

"Endure . . ." he whispered. "That's what he said.
And always strength comes for the task."

Searching silver eyes looked upon Gianavel.

"Is that the reason I was here? Was it so that I would
find the faith, the strength, to endure?"

Old and wise, the gray wolf nodded once, slowly.

"It was something I could not give. Only the
Lightmaker, in his grace, could lead you to this place.

Though had the beast struck you down once more, my wrath would have been his doom. But I stayed my strength, so that you might find yours, as I knew you would . . . in the end."

Then his father's voice grew solemn and grave, and he gazed tenderly at Saul's still form.

"Now he will run forever in fields green with laughter and light, where death has no dominion. And one day, too, you will run there beside him, friends forever."

Silently, gracefully, the old wolf then turned and walked toward the mountain trail that led north to home and safety and the comfort of the pack. At the trail he turned back again, his august form splashed with the golden dawn, to bid farewell. And even in the thin forest light Aramus could see love borne on the gaze of those deep gray eyes. Then with a whisper of the wind he vanished into the mist.

Aramus was alone with the dawning of the day. No longer did he feel his wounds, or his fears, or the cold that had chased him through the dark. And somehow, in his heart, he knew that he would never again fear the night. A quiet strength settled in his spirit as he turned to gaze at the southern treeline.

The mist still obscured the forest edge, but was thinning with the growing warmth of day. He did not know what dwelt beyond the distant woodline, but he knew his journey would be long. And after that, the long return home, to Lucas, and the pack, and a new life awaiting.

A single tear pierced the soft snow as the wounded wolf gently lifted his friend. And as the night's last stars slowly died in dawn's growing light, he turned solemnly south, and vanished into the mist as well.

Book Two

And if one
prevail against him,
two shall withstand him;
and a threefold cord
is not broken quickly.

o n e

Solemnly the great gray wolf poised atop his mountain domain. Gray eyes, wise and strong with ancient strength, gazed into the darkness as if to read the shadows, or the wind, or the moonlit night. And though the old wolf's shaggy mane waved slightly beneath the gusting breeze, he seemed unaware of the touch, the august head bent as if sensing a sad cry that carried faintly from some faraway place.

Silently, from the shadows that cloaked the cliff, another wolf stepped slowly into the moonlight. The wolf appeared older by far than the first, its gray mane blending white on the grizzled head and back. Yet though smaller in size than the massive creature it approached, the elder wolf moved with a lean, aged strength. And its hard, scarred face did not seem to know mercy or weakness, until it spoke, and the gray eyes softened with concern.

"The child has not returned, Gianavel?" asked Razul.

As if unable to look away from some distant foe, Gianavel shook his head. "No," he said, and sighed deeply, piercing the cold night air with his breath.

Gianavel continued to gaze into the distance, where sky and forest were lost beneath the conquering power of night, and his gray face hardened.

"We both know that the Lightmaker is doing a work in the child," said Razul. "And we both know that he must suffer much to gain his full strength. But you are troubled by something beyond this, brother. What is it you see in the night?"

Again Gianavel shook his head and gazed down the cliff beside them, seeming ready to descend the mountain with his thoughts.

"I don't know," he said softly. "I believe that the Lightmaker is working within my child. But it goes beyond that."

Razul said nothing, the ancient face tense. And together for a time they gazed, listening, into the night. Often Gianavel would raise his head, as if hearing something in the cold dark, but there was nothing. And although the great wolf did not move, his stance made lies of his stillness; a stance that spoke of fierce, savage strength, long held but now aroused, trembling to be unleashed.

Gianavel looked fully at Razul when he finally spoke again.

"I know that it is my place, as King of the Gray Wolves, to defend the pack. And rarely do I leave the mountain because of this. But now, for some reason, I am compelled in the spirit to find my son. I only hesitate because I sense that the pack is also in great danger. I'm not afraid to tell you, brother, that I'm troubled. Tell me what you see, Razul. Are we in agreement? Has an attack been launched against us?"

Gianavel's gray eyes searched for some assurance that his senses had not betrayed him. And Razul gazed back at him, the old eyes reflecting deep concern, but veiled from caution and long habit. Not quickly did the elder wolf reveal his mind, always weighing his words heavily; discerning, forever seeming to test his mortal thoughts against his matchless knowledge of the Truth. And Gianavel looked again across the darkened sky, waiting patiently, respecting the Elder's ancient wisdom, his august understanding of things past and present. Long ago, Gianavel had realized that even the future was not beyond the scope of Razul, so sensitive was he to the Lightmaker's spirit. The older wolf would speak when he would speak, and not before.

For a long time they watched from the high ridge, Gianavel focusing on the distant darkness, concentrating with hard gray eyes to read the night. And after a time, the wind altered its gusting pace, and he perceived a faint and grievous tone, a soft cry, subdued and saddened, as if the blood of all those crushed by cruelty were crying out to him from the earth; a cry that echoed with the endless pain forced upon the world by the Dark Lord. Gianavel lowered his head, sensing the suffering, the incomprehensible suffering inflicted since the dawn of time by that cruel hate. And as the wind died, leaving a grave stillness upon the high place, he heard Razul speak.

"It is said," the old voice rang clear and crisp in the cold air, "kill the head and the body will die. That is why the Dark Lord will try to destroy the greatest among us, and scatter the rest. You are King of the Gray Wolves, Gianavel. You are the strongest defender of the faith. And you are hated and feared by all who worship the Dark Lord. Even Baalkor fears you, knowing that the Lightmaker's spirit within you proclaims his doom. And because they fear you, they will kill you, if they can. I, too, sense that Aramus is in great danger, and you must go to him. You must go to him tonight. But I also sense that there is a great battle before us, a battle that will go far beyond your son. And I fear that we shall see much death before victory is won. For I perceive that the true plan of the Dark Lord is to destroy you, Gianavel, by somehow using your child against you. And when you are dead, the Dark Lord's servants hope to crush the faith from the Earth.

"My spirit compels me to warn you, brother. I know that you are strong, and your strength has delivered you many times in battle. But beware, for your strength can also destroy you. The Dark Lord is provoking you, even now, to strike back in your great anger, and wrath, hoping that you will betray the Lightmaker. For they know that if you are standing close to him they cannot defeat you. Yet they also know that if, somehow, they can cause you to forsake him, then you can be destroyed.

"I perceive in my spirit, I know in my heart, that this is the trap laid for you, Gianavel. But I will pray for you, as I have always prayed for you. And I know that you will overcome, even in this.

"Wisdom will guide you, my friend, wisdom gained from a long life of knowing and understanding the way of the Lightmaker. And with wisdom, remember your courage. These will deliver you from even the strongest attack. Then, when the battle has ended, as all our battles have ended before this, I hope that we will stand together again, as we stand now."

For a long moment Razul lifted his head, as if listening, or speaking. Then he looked again upon Gianavel, his ancient eyes keen and bright with knowledge and understanding.

"Unleash your strength, brother. The time of waiting has passed. Go, as the spirit within you compels you to go. And I will assemble the Elders, following at dawn."

Gianavel looked solemnly upon his old friend and nodded, his gray mane cloaked with an unflinching courage that seemed to transform him into a new creature. And the night grew still as the old king rose, standing dauntlessly beneath a dark wind that whispered of war and suffering and death.

For a breath Gianavel gazed down the steep cliff, its depths concealed within the swirling, chaotic darkness. And from somewhere within the gray eyes, a light, unearthly and unconquerable, emerged, defying the power of Night. Then, with a single movement, the great gray wolf moved boldly over the edge.

Like a thunderbolt Gianavel fell through the darkness, finding quick, narrow steps in the night, certain that his foot would not slip nor his courage fade, coming down from the mountain.

t w o

Alone in the white wilderness, high on a moonlit ridge, Aramus rested, searching for life in the forest night. Silent and still, he watched, and waited, while dark winds waved the shadowed trees and the pale moon cast frosty light across his high place.

After his journey south the Deep Woods had come alive with fiendish howls echoing long through the night. Dark wolves, enraged and vengeful from Baalkor's defeat, had quickly enclosed him within the forest. And the hunt had begun, a hunt that would never end until he was dead. Aramus understood the deadly game, and for past nights his cautious skills had evaded the demonic search. But it was a game that could not last. Sooner or later, he knew, he would make a mistake and they would trap him, as they had trapped his father long ago.

Often he had heard their vengeful howls pursuing his trail, and with the iron endurance of youth he had run relentlessly in ever-widening circles, crossing over his own tracks and circling again, exhausting and confusing his pursuers until the frustrated cries had faded into the night.

Afterwards, weary with his efforts, Aramus had thanked the Lightmaker for his escape, knowing that the spirit of the Living God had stood by his side, strengthening him. And knowing that survival depended on returning home, he had tried each night to slip through the wolf packs guarding the border of the Deep Woods. And each night he had failed, driven back again to the south by that killing zone.

Aramus breathed once, deeply, as he rested, and thought solemnly of Saul. He had never truly known death until that fateful night in the glade. And it troubled him, still. He had carried the grief with every step he had taken to the caves by the brook, where he had laid Saul. And when his promise to the old hare was finally fulfilled, the pain had become a deep wound in his soul, an inescapable emptiness within him. The wolf's heart weakened to think that never again would he speak with the old hare. Saul was gone, a life left behind. Now Aramus would have only what the future held. Despite his faith in the Lightmaker's promise, Aramus knew that each time he allowed his mind to return to those final few moments with Saul, he would know anew that sorrow of separation, a wound that would grow dim with days but endure for a lifetime.

Silver eyes closed as his heart gazed upon the lonely sight that had greeted him at the southern caves: the sight of the small, forlorn hares gathering sadly about the body of their fallen king. Aramus had watched the scene from a distance, his promise kept, his heart at peace.

The colony had stood a long time, solemn and weary, holding one another to ease the pain of their loss. And then, silently and strangely, they had parted, as one larger than the rest emerged from the caves. The big hare's dark fur was streaked with half-healed wounds, though he bore his pain bravely. And the others separated respectfully as he knelt beside Saul's still form, bowing their heads as one.

Even across the distance Aramus could see the sorrow that struck the massive figure. And here, he knew, was one who had loved his king much; a worthy son, a noble heir. A long time the big hare rested, silent and broken, his great form cloaked with his grief.

But as Aramus continued to watch, the hare suddenly started, as if sharply awakened from a dream, and raised his head. Aramus saw the bold, suspicious eyes quickly scan the glade and surrounding woodline. It took only a moment before the creature searched him out atop the distant hill. Then the hare stood up on its hind legs, instantly defiant, dark eyes focusing intently.

Aramus held the gaze, his silver eyes casting a sad shadow that seemed to span the separation between them. And as they stood, the hare's suspicious gaze slowly clouded with a strange and curious awe. It

dropped low, came forward a pace, and raised itself up
again, its eyes no longer challenging, but touched with a
searching hope. A long time they shared their sorrow,
each face reflecting a grievous loss, a solemn pain
beyond the expression of words or deeds. And then
slowly, carefully, Aramus lowered his head, revealing his
respect. The big hare seemed struck by the gesture, and
continued to return the gaze a moment more. Then he
also bent his head, once, and lowered himself again
upon his four paws.

The memory of that shared encounter had been the
single, bright place in Aramus's long journey. For he had
slept seldom, still disturbed and restless from his fright-
ful encounter in the Deep Woods, the deadly battle that
ended his long night in the storm.

Lost in the memory of that quiet encounter, Aramus
raised his head sharply as howls, unmerciful and hungry,
were hurled across the moonlit night. Action and
thought were one as he poised on the ridge, still and
alert, senses reaching out to test the air, the wind. And
almost instantly he knew that a chase was moving away
from him, lower into the hills. He frowned, listening
intently, strangely disturbed.

Not marked by the cold communication of a search,
the convening cries suddenly slashed the frosty night
with a malignant, merciless lust. Aramus recognized the
cries for what they were: the thrilling howls of killers
closing upon a kill. And from the manic, gleeful din, he
understood that the fiendish pursuit was near its end.

Making no sound, Aramus rose from the rocky ground. The howls were quickly gathering, not so far away. Then a roar shattered the night, not merciless or cruel, but fearful, enraged. The roar carried above the chaos of the hunt, superior for a moment before it was covered by a descending chorus of demonic cries.

Aramus began to step forward, his spirit reaching out to that tortured soul. But the old fear, that instinctive desire to preserve his own life above all else, immediately stilled his step. Then he remembered a snow-covered glade, and another wounded creature that had freely given far more than he had received, and Aramus smiled; a sad smile, but wise, and content with the knowledge that actions must follow faith, or faith is dead. And he stepped forward.

As a pale shadow Aramus moved quickly down the moonlit ridge and was soon gliding gracefully through the blackened corridors of the forest night, sensing the life of every creature he neared and moving away before it could know his spectral presence. With sure steps and unerring skill Aramus slowly increased his loping gait until he was running silently through the shadowy gloom, crossing the forest floor with supernatural grace, searching out the conflict with the gathering howls. And as he neared the ridge where the battle raged, Aramus instinctively slowed, moving even more carefully, alert to everything at once. Creatures hiding from the raging battle half-raised their heads as he neared, glimpsing the ghost of a wolf that never touched the earth, moving without sound through the forest night, and was gone.

Aramus reached the ridgecrest and waited, concealed within the shadows of the treeline. Gazing intensely across the wide, gray granite of the slope, he saw a swarm of dark wolves chasing a wounded bear. The wolves were closing upon the creature with hideous howls, and a quick glance revealed that the bear was near the end of its strength.

Torn by guilt, Aramus knew that he had been the true prey, but his stealth had eluded the pack's hateful search. And now, frustrated by his unending escape, the dark wolves had abandoned their hunt to turn upon any creature that crossed their path. Aramus watched, his brow furrowed with compassion, as the bear staggered up the rock-strewn slope, a brave and noble creature soon to die beneath those pursuing shapes. And he wondered if there would ever be an ending to this fight. The thought disturbed him, but he had no more time for thought. He knew that if he was to move, he must move quickly or not at all.

Even as Aramus thought, he slid silently from the concealing gloom of the woodline, gliding undetected across the ridge toward the bloodcurdling battle, choosing without hesitation to stand beside any creature who stood against that dark force.

♦ ♦ ♦

Wounded and weary, the bear stumbled up the moonlit

slope, breath heaving in hot blasts from his gasping mouth to cast a frightened glance over his shoulder. Behind him, emerging from the deeper gloom of the trees, he saw pairs of yellow eyes, fixed and hungry. The black shapes that followed moved more quickly then he, sliding as shadows from the darkness, their forms revealing no fatigue, no heaviness as the heaviness that weighed down his legs and caused him to stagger clumsily, pitifully, up the boulder-strewn hillside.

At dusk the dark army had descended from the hills, launching yet another attack upon him and his father. And he had fought bravely beside his sire until the old one fell, struck down by a great lion with eyes of flame.

His courage shattered by his father's death, the young bear had turned in panic, running blindly through the forest. And so he had run since dusk, staggering on and on through this strange land, weary and broken. But his desperate efforts were doomed; the wolves had remained apace, with stronger, fiercer ones taking the lead when the closest tired, continuously eroding his crumbling strength, leaving him easy prey for the fight.

Earlier, when the hellish horde had cornered him, he had turned, enraged, and struck sweeping blows with his great, curved claws. Two were crushed instantly, for even in his small frame there resided the awesome, inherent power of his kind. But during the savage encounter he had also been wounded, torn and slashed by the remaining predators who had descended upon him in a frenzy, shredding his dark fur and flesh.

Realizing with searing pain the futility of open combat, the bear had turned and fled as before, knowing that these were no ordinary wolves. Even with the howls that boomed through the night, he sensed that they were driven by some darker lust, some unearthly rage. And as he began to realize more clearly their deeper purpose, an indescribable horror had gripped his soul, a horror that whispered of cruel torment and suffering.

The beasts were nearly upon him again, he saw, with another backward glance. He neared the crest of a ridge, staggering beneath the weight of his fatigue, and ran toward two large boulders that could provide slight protection on his sides. Here, he knew, he would make his final stand. And even as he neared the rocks, he felt their hot breath upon him.

He reached the granite walls and turned, rising onto his hind legs and roaring a challenge that rattled dead leaves and shattered the night. The boldest, largest of the dark horde leapt upon him, and the bear struck savagely, his rage rising to overwhelm his horror. Then the pack was upon him, white fangs flashing viciously in the starlight, dark shapes leaping like shadows amidst the deafening din of war.

The bear defiantly stood his ground, roaring, striking crushing blows with his heavy paws, his last painful thoughts of the father he had lost in the wilderness, wishing the old bear were by his side.

three

Asweeping blow of the bear's paw struck a sadistic shape from the air, sprawling the wolf across the rock-strewn slope. But before the bear could see whether it lived or died, the others were upon him, covering him beneath a swirling storm of white fangs. He struck wildly in his rising fear and panic, his courage submerged beneath a wave of horror that shattered his instinct to fight.

One huge wolf collided against his legs, and the bear staggered, swaying against the roaring tide. And with a thunderous roar he fell, half-rolling on the steep incline. He lashed out blindly at his attackers as they flooded over him, a black sea of demonic forms and slavering fangs.

Malignant and horrible, one black wolf leapt upon his torn chest, its jaws horribly distended, prepared to draw deep blood. And the bear felt his last desperate hopes shatter with the sight.

Then a white avalanche of strength descended, roaring and striking, into the fray; a great silver shape that collided full against his snarling foe, sending the dark wolf careening wildly into the night. In a ferocious display of raw power the ghostly shape spun, a magnificent silver wolf, and struck another demonic shape that howled in agony and tore away.

As if suddenly resurrected from some nightmarish land of cruelty and despair, the bear roared, and with a volcanic effort threw off another fiendish form to gain his feet. Realizing instantly that what was not against him was for him, the bear stood shoulder to shoulder with the silver wolf, and the dark wolves were shaken by the sight.

Inspired by desperate hope and enraged by his searing wounds, the bear struck even more savagely than before. And the silver wolf also dealt deadly blows, striking like lightning to send two more of the dark pack staggering back with wounds.

In a moment it was over. As one, the fiendish pack broke away, howling and cursing in frustration, retreating as quickly as they had come. Angry cries followed the demonic horde as they raced down the ridge, fleeing into the night to merge chaotically with the darkness.

"Follow me!" shouted the silver wolf, and the wounded bear obeyed, too disoriented from the shock of combat to debate. And together, the silver shape leading, they ran across the ridge to fade into the treeline. The bear

trailed clumsily, his great weight smashing a wide,
bloody path through the forest.

A long time they ran, until the ridge was left far
behind and they arrived together, exhausted, beside a
wide, moonlit stream that rumbled soothingly beneath
outstretched branches of the shadowed night. Speechless
and fatigued, they rested.

Aramus lowered his head to drink from the stream,
and the bear followed his motion. They drank, and
rested, and drank still more until they felt their strength
returning. Finally, when Aramus had recovered from the
quick but savage battle, he stepped back from the stream
and gazed quietly at the bear.

During the frenzied battle on the ridge, Aramus had
only dimly noticed the creature's condition. But now he
saw that the bear was young, not even half-grown, still
far from the size and strength it would command with
age. Yet it was already strong in its wrath, and could be
dangerous to arouse. Even though he had saved its life,
Aramus remained cautious, knowing from experience
that the quick, native temper of the creature was easily
provoked. With a safe distance between them, he
regarded it carefully, prepared to flee if need arose.

Finally, its great thirst satisfied, the bear also stepped
back wearily and turned to look upon him. Its haggard
face was confused and drawn from long despair. And
suddenly, as if unable to stand, the bear laid down, its
open mouth heaving great breaths. Aramus continued to
watch silently, studying its cuts bleeding black in the

white light of night. The bear seemed weary unto death, and Aramus waited for the creature to compose himself.

And when it was quiet and rested, seeming to find some peace in this quiet place, he spoke.

"I am Aramus, son of Gianavel."

Still breathing heavily, the bear stared at him, tired and sad, and its mind seemed far away. Fresh pain welled within the soft brown eyes as the creature spoke.

"I am Kaleel," he whispered. "They killed my father."

Aramus felt a piercing sorrow for the creature, and he lowered his head, grieving that his battle in the Deep Woods could have led to such senseless pain. But he was becoming accustomed to death, even death that claimed lives of the innocent.

"I am . . . sorry," he said softly. "They were hunting me. Not you. You only fell into the trap."

The young bear stared at him a moment longer, grieving and broken. Then it shook its head wearily.

"No," he whispered weakly. "My father has fought with the dark wolves before. They hated him because he loved the Lightmaker. It was the lion—"

Aramus ceased to breathe.

"Incomel?" he asked softly.

The bear studied him a moment, seeming to grow even more weary and sad. He lowered his gaze to the ground.

"Yes . . . Incomel. He hated my father. He was with the wolves when they attacked. Even as my father died, he told me to run. So . . . I ran. I . . . didn't know . . . what else to do."

Aramus looked into Kaleel's tired face. He started to speak again, but the eyes of his heart suddenly looked upon another scene: a scene of death far from this place, where snow had laid deep and an ancient beast had stalked forth from a storm; a scene where a dying hare had shared the pain of a frightened wolf until the wolf had shared its strength. Aramus breathed deeply with the memory, knowing again every emotion, every word spoken during the long night that would live forever within him.

Shining silver eyes gazed carefully at the bear. Aramus knew that if he moved quickly and alone he could cross the border in the confusion of this latest conflict, long before the dark wolves reassembled their strength. Yet with the bear at his side, wounded and slow, escape was less likely. But even as he stared at the creature, feeling its pain, he knew that he could not withhold his help. He almost sensed a burden lifting from his shoulders as he spoke, as if he had made a grave decision, though he had made the decision so quickly, and so easily, that it was hardly a decision at all.

"You can come with me," Aramus said, sensing the price he would pay. "And we'll cross the border together. If we move quickly we can be on my father's mountain by tomorrow night. The dark wolves won't go there. They're afraid of the Elders of the Gray Wolves. And you'll be safe. We won't harm you."

Kaleel gazed at him. "You will help me?"

Despite the great, sudden weariness that overwhelmed his own soul, Aramus smiled.

"I'll help you."

◆ ◆ ◆

Gianavel sped through the night that seemed as day, so clearly did he see the land that rolled away beneath him, white and dark in the moonlight.

The great gray wolf descended a steep slope, gathering speed with each hurtling stride to reach the base. Then his powerful legs transformed the speed into grace, launching him up the next ascent with wide bounds. He cleared the crest, found level ground, and stretched out his long stride, scorning the endless miles, fiercely enduring the pain that burned in his limbs.

In time, he knew, the weight of mortal flesh would make him slow his speed to a loping gait that he could maintain for days. But for now his strength could not be contained, his spirit and endless love compelling him to find his child.

He hurled himself through the darkened corridors of the forest night, racing with the wind, reading every shadow to find the surest path to the south. And even as he ran, he prayed, asking for strength equal to the task.

Suddenly a dark panorama arose in the great wolf's mind: a ghastly vision of his loyal pack lying bloody and dying on a snowy mountainside, their strength broken, their faith crushed. And Aramus, too, laid in that haunting scene, torn and dying beside the father who had come so swiftly to rescue him.

Enraged, Gianavel roared, even as he ran, knowing the thoughts were not his own, refusing to allow the Dark Lord a stronghold in his heart. And channeling his great, thrilling anger into strength, the gray wolf leaped forward with a speed that devoured the distance before him, defeating the darkness with the fierceness of his faith.

four

Aramus awoke, not certain he had ever slept. He vaguely remembered a long, troubled night dozing fitfully beside the rumbling stream with shattered dreams of red death in a snowy field, a demonic lion with eyes of flame standing before him, and a colossal, darkened cave that held something monstrous... waiting. ...

He stood, blinking, and shook the cold from his damp mane. Kaleel was beside him, breathing deeply in heavy sleep. Aramus regarded the bear carefully in the faint starlight of early morning. The dark patches in its fur were ravaged, its flesh torn, yet there was no killing wound.

Instinctively moving without sound, Aramus made his way back along the trail they had followed in their desperate escape. And he saw that the path was crushed, marked with blood, an easy trail to track. He followed the wide swath for a short distance, becoming more alert as he moved. His eyes constantly shifted from the trail to the forest ahead, scanning the shadowed trees, listening, watching. But his movements did not require conscious thought, so completely had he been transformed in the ordeal of past days. Without thinking he did what he had to do, always searching, always alert. But he found no scent, no marks, no sign of a pursuing pack. And he began to feel somewhat easier as he stalked through the golden light of dawn. Until he thought of his father.

With a disturbing intensity, Aramus was suddenly concerned for the old wolf. Gianavel would be worried by now and might even be searching for him in the Deep Woods. Aramus hoped that his father had not ventured south. He was a hated enemy of the Dark Council, and was always in great danger when he came down from the mountain.

Even before Aramus felt the gentle breeze that bore it, a sudden scent assaulted his senses. Mane bristling, he froze in his silent stride. And for a long moment he stood, searching, before realizing that the beast was still far away.

Confused, Aramus could not immediately identify the scent. It did not emanate from any creature he had ever known. Though dimly, submerged somewhere within the windblown presence, there resided the faint trace of a lionlike force, as if what had once been a lion had been hellishly transformed into something more, something hideous and monstrous and bloodthirsty, something the earth was never meant to endure.

Quickly Aramus turned and backtracked through the forest, heedless of the slight sound caused by his haste. He knew somehow that stealth would not save them now. Their only chance rested upon speed and endurance. In a moment he was at the stream, where Kaleel was sitting up, gazing at him with curious eyes.

"They are coming," Aramus whispered. "I think Incomel is with them. We must move quickly."

Instantly the bear was on his feet, instinctively swaying from side to side, displaying his distinctive shape and stance to any enemy approaching. Aramus knew the movement and replied quickly, quietly.

"No. They are not close. But they'll be here soon. We've got to move fast."

Then Aramus was loping along the stream, moving toward the golden sun, Kaleel shambling close behind. And as they ran, the stream narrowed, the rocks growing larger and more shattered until only huge, jagged pieces of granite lay alongside the stream.

On and on they ran, and as they moved higher up the stream the banks began to steepen, ascending quickly, until they were enclosed by two towering granite walls. Aramus did not like being trapped by the impassable cliffs, and saw that it had been foolish to follow the stream for so long. Now they were trapped, with retreat impossible. Aramus realized bitterly that he had made a mistake that could cost them their lives.

Unable to retreat, they continued onward, leaping from boulder to boulder, moving quickly, always searching for a way out of the narrow canyon. And finally, when the cold sun was high, Aramus saw a thin break in the monolithic granite wall on the opposite shore. The narrow crevice seemed strangely unnatural, as if some irresistible force had descended upon the stone with devastating impact, shattering the cliff and leaving behind a thin slash of broken rock.

"We have to go that way," Aramus said, looking back at Kaleel. "If we don't get off this streambed, they'll catch us. But if we climb that cliff we can get into open country, and then we can go north. Do you think you can make it?"

Kaleel cast an exhausted glance toward the cliff. Aramus knew that the bear preferred to stand and fight, not accustomed to fleeing a foe. But escape was their only chance. If Incomel was really stalking them, the beast could kill the son as quickly as he had killed the father.

Kaleel nodded, breathing hard. "I think so," he said wearily.

Aramus leapt first into the freezing water, instantly shocked by the killing cold that enveloped his flesh. Swimming strongly, using the fierce movements to fight off the deathlike chill, he quickly crossed the fast-flowing stream. And in a moment he raised himself upon the opposite shore, shaking violently to throw the invading cold from his shaggy coat. Kaleel emerged a moment later, heavy with the fatigue of his wounds.

Standing in the shadow of the towering ridge,
Aramus felt a disturbing pall of fear. As he gazed up the
cliff, a trembling, not caused by the cold, began in his
legs. And with the trembling came a weary heaviness, a
rising fatigue that loomed like a wave within him. Was
this truly how it was going to be? Was a life of faith
always going to be one fierce challenge after another,
one fight after another, conflict upon conflict,
struggling always to overcome both his fears and the
darkness of the world?

With a sad shadow dimming his silver eyes, Aramus
remembered how Saul, so small in strength, yet so great
in spirit, had remained faithful and true to the end,
despite his pain, despite the agony of his wounds. And
he knew he would do the same. The battle was
unending, and with each new struggle he would have to
allow the spirit of the Lightmaker to master his fears
again, strengthening him for the task. With the thought,
the wolf set his jaw with an effort of will that focused
his vision to a narrow view, setting nothing before him
but the challenge of ascending the path.

"Let's go," Aramus said softly and stepped forward.
"We overcome or we die."

Freezing and wet, the rocky face was slippery and
hazardous to negotiate. Even with his superior sureness
of step, Aramus was forced to carefully avoid uncertain
footholds. Halfway up the treacherous climb, he glanced
down and saw that Kaleel was struggling fiercely in his
halting efforts to ascend the bluff. The bear's wide dark
paws, with their huge, curved claws, scraped desperately

at the slanting granite. And after each abrupt movement
the bear would stretch prone upon the freezing rock,
grasping tenaciously at narrow holds, snatching brief
moments of rest.

On trembling legs Aramus ascended to the last,
steepest section of the bluff and saw that there was no
place to step. A small overhang, smooth as blackened
bone, descended in a curtain from the rim. Aramus
carefully studied the glistening edge, measuring its
distance. Then he glanced cautiously down at the
streambed below. A killing fall.

Always strength comes for the task, he told himself.
Always strength comes for the task. But his legs continued
to tremble, and his breath came fast and deep as he
struggled to control his fear.

He looked at the rim again. When, he wondered,
would he command the strength that Saul had commanded, that Gianavel commanded? Aramus knew that
his father would never be afraid of this. Gianavel would
clear this and be gone. But Aramus knew he did not
have the strength of his father, and he feared that he
never would.

With silver eyes focused intently on the black rim,
Aramus crouched, tensing his powerful legs, and
launched himself upwards. A long moment he sailed
through the air, enveloped by the wind, then landed
lightly on the summit. Even as his paws touched level
ground, Aramus surged with exultation. Unable to
contain his joy, he ran a few steps down the slope ahead
before turning back to the cliff.

Looking over the edge, he saw that Kaleel was almost halfway up the wall, his breath heaving in huge, vaporous clouds from his gaping mouth. The weariness of the bear concerned Aramus. They would cover little ground before nightfall. Warily, he looked down the stream, but there was no sign of the dark pack, no movement along the water, now blindingly white in the sun.

Vaguely confused, knowing that the pack should have been upon them by now, Aramus turned to gaze across the sloping glade at his back. Only hills could be seen beyond, strangely haunting, bleak and soundless. And there was no movement of life, no song or cry or the faintest flutter of wings in all the desolation.

Silver eyes narrowed as he studied the sight. Something was wrong here, he knew, something he could not place. And he felt a curious impression, a disturbing premonition that warned him not to enter that land. But he had no time to ponder the thought.

He looked back to Kaleel, who had finally scraped his way to the same precipitous piece of granite that Aramus had cleared. The bear stood on the last flat foothold, studying the edge with quick breaths. Aramus saw Kaleel's great brown form trembling from the fear and effort of struggling up the cliff. Frustrated, the bear swung his head nervously from side to side, desperately searching the rock for a way of escape and becoming more fearful by the moment.

Aramus saw the thick legs brace, as if to chance a wild leap for the summit, and realized instantly that the bear would not survive. And even as Aramus saw the movement, he shouted.

"No!"

five

Wait," Aramus said, more softly.

Kaleel looked desperately to Aramus, to the rock, and back again, seemingly unable to contain his fearful energy. Then he sat back, his head bent with fatigue, white mist steaming slowly with each heated breath.

Aramus paced the edge, studying the situation. It was not good. If Kaleel missed the leap, he would never survive the fall. Aramus concentrated, searching for the right words, praying for wisdom. What had he learned during this long ordeal? What had Saul told him when he was so afraid? Aramus closed his eyes, breathing deeply. And as he waited, his thinking cleared.

"Kaleel, listen," he began, careful to keep his voice calm, deliberate. "You've got to control yourself before you do anything else. You've got to think clearly. Just rest for a moment. Get your strength back. Calm down."

Kaleel seemed to be listening, leaning against the granite face, his breath slowing, more measured and sure. Aramus could see the dark eyes studying the narrow edge, and he spoke again in a soothing voice.

"Even if you don't jump, I'm not going to leave you. I'll come down and we'll find another way out of this. So don't worry. Just concentrate on what you have to do, and do it. But when you jump, forget your fear, forget your life. Just do what you have to do. Do it with all your might. And the Lightmaker will do the rest. Trust me."

Kaleel looked up at Aramus, his brown eyes frightened, but trusting. And Aramus smiled, nodding encouragement. Then the bear shifted his gaze to the rocky ledge, and Aramus could see him concentrating, breathing slowly, gathering his strength. The tense gaze centered with renewed focus on the lowest dip in the ledge. The heavy legs braced.

A violent shove launched the bear skyward, and the huge front paws slapped over the edge. For an agonizing moment hind feet scraped savagely against the smooth granite, gashing white marks in the stone. Then with one long, laborious effort, Kaleel hauled himself onto the summit, collapsing clumsily on the level ground.

Aramus's heart thrilled at the sight, and he leaped to the bear's side.

"I knew you could do it!" he shouted.

Kaleel nodded, seemingly unable to consider anything but the heavy weariness in his flesh and the exalting relief of finishing the climb. He sprawled on the ridge, panting. And Aramus saw the physical pain of deep wounds in the brown eyes. It seemed that in his great relief, Kaleel had forgotten completely about the fiendish pack that was pursuing them.

Aramus turned to watch the gorge below, studying every shadow that waved and shifted along the rocky stream. He knew that, in time, when the bear grew into his full strength, he would climb the cliff more easily than any creature living.

All strength comes in time, he thought, as he looked again at the tired, panting form. Endurance is gained by enduring.

"Feeling stronger?" Aramus asked, after a moment.

Kaleel nodded, having recovered slightly. He looked at Aramus, focusing, as if truly seeing the wolf for the first time.

"Thank you," he said in a weary voice, but calmer than Aramus had heard it before. "I didn't think... I'd make it."

Aramus laughed. "We're always stronger than we think."

Kaleel stared at him, wonder touching his weariness.

"You are brave," he said.

Aramus continued to smile, and then the silver eyes blinked slowly.

"No," he said quietly. "Not brave. I know fear a lot better than I know courage. Not too long ago I thought that my days of fear were over. But now I know that it never truly ends. Flesh is flesh and will always rise up.

But I'm a lot stronger than I used to be. Now I just want to live what I believe—"

Aramus hesitated, his face suddenly more noble, more beautiful, yet sad with a sadness that transcended words. Kaleel sensed the change, the solemn pain that descended upon the silver brow.

"What is it?" the bear asked.

Aramus lowered his head, as if his thoughts were too much to endure, too much altogether.

"But there's a price to pay for living what you believe," the wolf said softly, and closed his eyes. "I have seen the bravest fall... the bravest... the best."

Kaleel rested beside the wolf, not understanding the words but finding peace and strength in the companionship.

Aramus shook his head.

"I wasn't ready for this," he said. "I've made too many mistakes. It was right to stand beside you on the hill, but we shouldn't have rested. We should have pushed on through the night. We could have made it to the North. And we shouldn't have followed the stream for so long. It trapped us and led us to this place."

Aramus looked again at the land before them. The sun was still high, but its fierce heat did not descend upon the rocky edge of the chasm. The place seemed remote from the world, submerged beneath a separate chill that conquered the day with disturbing strength. Aramus studied the forest cautiously. The trees seemed cloaked with a defiant cold, a cold that refused to retreat before the light of day. It was almost as if they stood beside a vast, eternal grave, shrouded by a pale darkness, invisible with the day but which would come alive with the night, ruling this dying land.

"I don't even know where we are," Aramus said quietly. "I've never seen this part of the Deep Woods before, and I don't like it. There's no life in this place. Nothing. Maybe we can—"

Howling fiendishly a dark wolf leaped over the edge of the chasm. Aramus roared and twisted desperately to evade the form, but its jaws tore a deep wound in his side. Howling, Aramus staggered back and fell, realizing bitterly that he had made even another mistake by failing to maintain a lookout on the gorge below.

He saw the next two movements as if they were one. The snarling black shape leaped upon him again, and then Kaleel was there, roaring and leaping forward in a single motion to strike the demonic shape full across the breast, impaling it upon his great, curved claws. The bear's mountainous strength continued the blow, hurling the creature far over the edge of the ravine, and a dying howl descended with the beast.

Instantly Aramus was on his feet.

"Run!" he shouted, sensing injury and defeat together, cursing himself for his carelessness. But Kaleel was already charging down the slope.

Aramus leaped to the cliff to chance a quick glance over the edge and caught the shocking sight of dark wolves swarming up the granite face, sinister in their silent attack.

Instantly Aramus was after Kaleel, feeling in his heart that doom was upon them. He passed the bear before it reached the trees, and turned back to see another dark shape leap atop the cliff. As the wolf caught sight of them, it unleashed a horrendous howl that boomed down the slope, reverberating against the dead trees.

"Hurry!" Aramus shouted. Kaleel thundered past him, sweeping into the forest, and together they ran, searching for a defensive position as more cries blasted from the ridge. And in moments they burst through the barren stand, emerging into a small clearing dominated by a low, windswept hill.

"We'll fight them on the hill!" Aramus shouted.

They climbed the low ascent until they stood on the highest tactical ground, ready to meet the bloody assault. And together they turned as they reached the crest to behold malignant black forms exploding from the desolate stand, howls blasting through the glade.

Enraged, Aramus snarled savagely at the onrushing pack, and Kaleel towered upon hind legs, lowering his head to roar thunderously. The bear struck eagerly at the air, foam flecking the fiercesome, gaping fangs, its great strength aroused once more.

Slowing at the base of the hill, the wolves advanced as one force, rolling forward in a black tide of hated shapes.

Kaleel's first great blow caught a fiendish form in midair, hurling the dark creature aside. And Aramus tensed to charge at an advancing wolf, prepared to die beside his friend, when suddenly he felt something attacking from behind. Aramus whirled, far ahead of conscious thought, to glimpse a gigantic lion, if lion it could be called, descending upon Kaleel.

Sensing the attack, the bear spun, paws uplifted to strike. Yet even as Kaleel saw the horrific beast descending upon him, he staggered back, as if struck by some unseen force. The lion's massive foreleg appeared to lash out, too quick to follow with sight, and Kaleel's head was hit with a thunderous blow. As dead, the bear sprawled across the slope, a roar dying in his throat.

Aramus cried out as Kaleel rolled down the hillside, broken and unconscious, but he was unable to determine if his friend was dead or alive. Then Aramus had no more time to think as the lion turned toward him, and he knew its identity.

Incomel.

Aramus's silver eyes hardened above a defiant snarl.

More powerful, more loathsome than any mountain lion Aramus had ever known, the beast advanced with sinuous, measured steps. Massive and black, the huge rolling muscles of its gigantic form coiled and swelled with each imperious step, flexing with unimaginable strength; strength never used and never needed to destroy anything that lived. And an aspect of violence cloaked its entire essence; a visible violence born from violent needs and flamed hot by the pure release of deadly force, and death. The beast advanced until it stood before Aramus, horrible in its stillness, even its

motionless stance whispering of unearthly power and
strength.

The lion's gaze burned, shifting in shades, as if a
thousand demonic lights danced within. Then it tilted
its massive head and spoke.

"So . . . we stand against each other," the deep voice
intoned, echoing with suppressed strength. "A brave
servant of the Lightmaker and a poor, deceived servant
of the Dark Lord. Which one of us shall leave this
lonely place?"

Aramus said nothing, but he knew this was the end
of his life. His hopes were as dead as he soon would be.

Incomel laughed, leaving even the daylight distant
and pale with its malignant presence. Aramus sensed
that the wind had fallen still, as if held back by some
sinister force.

Aramus searched for words to signal his defiance, but
all he could remember were those closest to his heart;
his fiercest faith, his strongest love. For all else passed
away before the beast.

"I am Aramus," he said, "son of Gianavel, a servant
of the Lightmaker. And—"

Incomel snarled, trembling the ground beneath them.
Aramus instinctively dropped lower in his stance,
snarling in return, flaming with fear.

Incomel laughed mockingly. "What do you believe?"
it rasped.

Aramus saw nothing but the great, distended fangs.
Fearfully he weighed his words before he spoke.

"I am a servant . . . of the Lightmaker."

Aramus never saw the blow that struck him, but the thunderous impact hurled him from the ridge. In the next instant he was sprawling wildly down the hillside, spinning and careening off dark wolves who scattered beneath his chaotic descent. Then he reached the base, crashing heavily into a granite slab.

Dazed and disoriented, Aramus staggered blindly to his feet, unable to find the direction from which he had come. He stood on shocked legs, struggling painfully for breath, even as a lancing wound pierced his side. He swayed unsteadily, catching brief, shallow snatches of air with each heaving effort. And through a red haze he saw Incomel standing before him again.

Its malevolent eyes burned with sadistic pleasure, measuring his agony. And its quiet words seethed with hate.

"What do you believe?"

Aramus blinked, barely beginning to catch his breath, and he felt his ribs bleeding from the piercing talons. Without thought a snarl distorted his face as he cast his words.

"I am . . . a servant—"

Aramus saw the blow this time and spun sideways. But Incomel was lightning, and the great force caught him across the neck. For a whirling, timeless instant Aramus felt as if he had been snatched up by a storm, spun through the air in a twisting wind, and smashed against the earth. He did not know how he landed, or where, but the bruising concussion left him dazed, on his side, his silver mane covered with dust. Dimly conscious, unable to speak, unable to think, Aramus struggled numbly to his feet. And saw the lion before him again, its eyes glimmering with cruel mirth.

Painfully, Aramus shook his head, shocked, and could not return the stare. He lowered his head, struggling to breathe again, swaying unsteadily. He felt as if his strength had been obliterated by those colossal blows, his thoughts scattered like leaves in the wind. He tried to focus, raised his head with an effort, and beheld the demonic gaze directed hatefully upon him.

Aramus did not want to remove his eyes from the lion's monstrous shape, but he chanced a quick glance toward Kaleel. The bear was staggering up slowly from the cold ground, casting frightened and stunned looks about, as if searching for the horrendous beast that had struck him down. And though Incomel seemed aware of the bear's movements, it did not turn.

"Corbis has instructed me to bring you to the mountain," it growled, its jagged jaws threatening Aramus for a long, chilling instant, its guttural roar trembling the ground beneath them. "So you will come with me, or I will destroy you. Do you understand?"

Aramus knew he would live or die with his words. He glanced again at Kaleel, saddened that his poor leadership had brought them to this peril. Then he looked again to Incomel, who stood ready to drench the barren ground with their blood.

"And the bear?" asked Aramus.

Incomel threw a cold glance at Kaleel.

"He dies. Like his father."

Aramus hesitated, understanding for the first time the true advantage of tactics in this cruel war. He knew that Incomel feared Corbis, the one creature even more terrible in its wrath. And Aramus realized that, with cunning, perhaps there was something to be gained. He looked fully into the lion's glowering gaze.

"Bring the bear with us, and I will go," he said. "But if you harm him, I will fight, and you'll have to kill me. And that will not please Corbis."

Incomel's growl rumbled in its deep throat, though its stance remained scornful and imperious. Then it smiled, although the jagged grimace never reached the murderous gaze.

"So . . . you will outsmart poor Incomel?"

Aramus said nothing.

And Incomel laughed: a roaring, demonic laugh that caused Aramus's mane to bristle. For a moment the beast roared on in its mirth, until the laughter died, and it heaved a deep breath of the pale air, enjoying its amusement.

"At least you have spirit," it intoned, and paused a moment longer. Then it looked at the sky, setting defiant eyes against the heavens.

"The bear may come with you," it said, regarding Aramus once more. "Whether I kill one of you, or both, does not matter to me. But I don't want to drag your dead body all the way to the Abyss."

Incomel turned to Kaleel.

"Come."

For the briefest moment Kaleel seemed ready to test his strength once more against the lion. The bear's dark eyes focused intently on the beast, struggling to contain some devastating rage, some vengeful wrath that threatened to overcome his control.

Kaleel's face seemed as stone when he spoke.

"The Lightmaker will make you pay for my father's death," he growled.

Incomel's gaze revealed nothing.

A moment more did the tension last, with Incomel poised to strike a blow that would kill like lightning. Kaleel cast a smoldering look toward Aramus, who shook his head sharply. And finally, slowly, the bear lowered his gaze to the ground, and Aramus nodded, breathing easier. He knew that the Lightmaker might yet provide a chance to overcome this cruel enemy. But not here, and not now.

Undisturbed by the bear's challenge, Incomel turned and moved menacingly down the hill, casting a despising glance toward the fiendish pack as if it might slay them together with a look. The wolves cringed as one, falling silently back.

Kaleel and Aramus followed brokenly in the lion's wake, and in a moment they were enveloped by the desolate land; a disturbing, evil land that stretched into nothingness, silent and dead, tomblike and still, as if everything living had been slain together and crushed into dust by some hellish force, and the land alone remained, mourning its loss of life.

◆   ◆   ◆

Unseen and unheard, the burly shape rose cautiously from behind the cluster of boulders bordering the glade, gazing intently at the silver shape being led away.

Windgate had not known what had compelled him to leave the safety of the caves earlier in the day. He only knew that he had felt driven to venture north into this oppressive wilderness, greatly troubled in spirit. And now, with the savage battle he had just witnessed he sensed that, at last, the true reason for his mysterious journey was clear.

Windgate knew that the silver wolf had somehow stood beside Saul in his death, for the wolf had brought Saul's body home from the Deep Woods. And now the wolf was a prisoner of those same dark forces that had killed Saul. Windgate frowned as he watched the pack disappearing into the forest. And he knew that a debt of service remained; a debt that he would pay for his fallen king.

Even as Windgate watched, fearfully weighing the heavy task before him, he shifted in his quiet stance. It would not be easy to help the silver wolf; unknown dangers and unlimited powers were locked in some conflict that might well destroy the land. And he was no match for wolves. But even as the big hare considered the precious price he might pay, he laughed scornfully, knowing that he would never retreat from those who had slain Saul.

For a brief moment more Windgate waited, until the dark shapes were lost in the distant trees, pursuing a narrow trail far into the Deep Woods. Then he stepped slowly forward, moving from behind his place of concealment with cautious grace.

Without cover he crossed the clearing, knowing that any casual, backwards glance from the disappearing pack would instantly reveal his presence. But his choice was made, his way clear. And in a moment he had crossed the small glade, defiantly following the silver wolf into an immense and foreboding forest of graves.

s i x

Gianavel relentlessly tracked the faint scent, following the trail across wide fields of melting snow, through ragged forests, spectral and haunting in the haggard light of the moon, until day had dawned with a crimson sun. And still, unresting and unyielding, the old wolf steadfastly pursued the path that would take him to his son.

Gray and massive in the ascending sun, Gianavel tracked with every skill of his long years, making no sound, leaving no sign and always careful the wind did not carry his scent before him. On and on the old wolf moved with ghostly stealth, sacrificing haste for caution. He was increasingly anxious to find his son, but his disciplined mind would not forget wisdom and patience. Instead, he grew even more methodical, channeling his great concern into his strength, allowing no rest, wasting no time, and missing nothing that marked the faint trail.

With long bounds he followed it up the shattered granite cliff that bordered a stream to emerge cautiously on the summit, for experience warned him that the narrow ledge was a likely spot for an ambush, but as he landed, ready to meet any threat, he saw that he was alone.

Not persuaded so quickly, Gianavel stood listening, reading the terrain before him, a frown darkening his face. The land stretched out with gravelike stillness, and the old wolf knew he stood near the center of the Deep Woods. And though he met no attack, he felt a sinister sensation, a sensation of disturbing intensity. He scowled, glaring into the surrounding forest, observing nothing but perceiving a deadly and faintly familiar threat in the pale air. He sensed something unearthly was close beside him, or had passed this way not long before. And the knowledge frightened him, for he knew that Aramus had also come this way.

Cautiously he moved down the hill, tracking his son, until he came into a small clearing dominated by a low hill. Head bowed and eyes wary, Gianavel moved to the hill, searching, searching. And in moments he found the blood of his son, beside the scent of . . . Incomel.

Even as he found his son's blood and the hellish scent, Gianavel's great fangs emerged in a rumbling snarl, and the gray eyes smoldered, like thunderclouds struggling to contain the storm within. He scanned the

surrounding woodline, hoping there would indeed be an
ambush so that he might release his anger. But there was
nothing. Only tracks that led on into the forest, toward
the heart of the Deep Woods—the Abyss.

For a long, tense moment Gianavel stood, breathing
heavily in his wrath, until his spirit began to still his
blood, enabling him to think clearly. Strength would not
deliver, he knew. Flesh would never prevail against
spiritual forces more powerful than flesh.

Briefly Gianavel closed his eyes, searching his heart,
communing with the spirit of the Lightmaker who had
long ago graced him with wisdom and strength. Then,
staring across the desolation, his mind suddenly filled
with the image of the son he loved more than life. The
old wolf's love for his child was like a mortal wound,
and his breath caught in his massive chest, pained to
know that his son had been crushed by the cruel power
of the Beast. And Gianavel bowed his head, enduring
his wounding grief.

A long time the great gray wolf stood, head lowered,
while the lonely darkness thickened about him and the
Lightmaker's spirit rose within, strengthening his heart
as it had strengthened him for long years past. Gianavel
nodded, knowing his God as he would know an old
friend, finding all that he sought in that sacred life.
And when the sun had descended well below the
soundless horizon, the old wolf raised his head again.

Silently Gianavel moved into the darkened forest,
hunting as before, with head bowed and eyes wary. And
then, slowly, he increased his pace until he eased into a

loping gait. Glades and streams and distant hills grew
visible, neared, and passed, but his endurance did not
waver. Driven by the power within him, the old wolf
increased his speed even more, and more, until he ran
with powerful, leaping strides that mysteriously knew no
fatigue and no pain, carrying him through the darkness
with unerring skill, releasing the full measure of a
strength that hurled his ghostly shape through the night
like the wrath of a vengeful God, coming to deliver
justice to the Earth.

◆ ◆ ◆

Light died beneath a darkness that began long before
the sun descended upon the foreboding, oppressive hills.
Aramus had felt the heaviness of the night even as he
traveled through the light, disturbed and confused by
the endless sea of nothingness that enveloped him on all
sides. In every place he looked, sweeping into the
distance, he saw no living creature, no green leaf. Even
the fallen limbs that covered the land like a gray,
wrinkled blanket were dry and wasted from long death.
The entire forest was drained of life, as if all beauty, all
hope, had been mercilessly crushed from everything that
lived.

Desperate for encouragement and strength, Aramus
thought back to the battle in the glade when Saul had
stood beside him, and he struggled to remember all he
had learned from the heroic hare. But somehow, Saul's
wisdom was drowned out by the chaos within his mind.

Broken in heart and hope, Aramus moved onward with the menacing escort. Step by step, he was worn down by his doubts, his guilt, as they journeyed across the vast landscape that stretched, barren and desolate, into only more nothingness. As far as he could see there was silence, with solemn forests marking an endless grave. Not even a sparrow or swallow could be heard in the gray evening light.

Unearthly, unreal and unendurable, the land oppressed him. And as they journeyed ever deeper into the foreboding darkness, Aramus felt something within him growing colder and more distant from that source of strength he had cherished only days before, his weakness made greater by the knowledge that he would soon stand before Corbis.

Together the thoughts tore at his heart until he felt an overwhelming panic rising in his soul, a panic of dread expectation. In agony he remembered his father, who might even now be searching for him. But even as that desperate hope strengthened his heart, the voice of raging, screaming doubt rose in his mind, telling him that Gianavel would never find him, or even dare to follow him into this ghastly land. And in moments Aramus was convinced that, perhaps, it was true: he was lost and alone in this hateful place.

In his suffering Aramus knew the true weaknesses of his flesh, understanding how much within his heart remained like the land surrounding him, saddened and starving for the force that would give it life. Yet in his spirit, through some last, surviving sense that defied the gathering gloom, Aramus perceived that, even as a deeper life and victory had been delivered unto him in his battle with Baalkor, a deeper life and victory would also be delivered to him in this persecution, if he would only hold to what he believed.

With each weary stride Aramus had watched a mountainous glacier of black ice, crowned by darkened storm clouds, coming closer. Now, as the sun finished its slow descent, they began to climb the steep path that led to the icy dome, Aramus following in a daze until the ground lay hidden beneath the hardening ice and steadily falling snow.

Aramus knew that they were climbing above the treeline where nothing but rocks and snow and ice could endure. Everything around him was as hard and sharp as the black ice that hung from the sweeping cliffs, lending an indescribable aspect of doom. Aramus faltered, stumbling, as his wounds and deep fatigue weighed him down and the trail grew more difficult. He was tired now and needed to rest, but he could not rest, driven on by these cruel creatures of darkness.

On and on they climbed, slashed by the lightning and ice that descended hatefully from the darkness crowning the nightmarish peak. The storm seemed eternal, and Aramus had to force himself to walk, shivering beneath the embracing arctic air that grew colder with each tortured step. He concentrated on climbing, his exhausted gaze fixed solidly before him, his numb mind focusing on his efforts. A long time he continued at his bone-weary pace, oblivious to how far they traveled or how high they climbed, following whatever dark shape moved before him, dark shapes that seemed to grow stronger and fiercer with each step they took toward the icy summit.

Yet as they crossed a jagged section of black granite, Aramus lifted his head, suddenly sparked by a dynamic, mysterious strength. Despite his fatigue, the silver wolf raised his eyes to see that the trail ran directly beneath a wide ledge, flat and black in the rising moon. The ledge towered commandingly above the path and seemed accessible only by way of a steep slope that glistened with dark ice. Strangely curious, Aramus studied the gloomy precipice, silver eyes memorizing every wrinkle of the expansive ridge. Then, as suddenly as the mysterious strength had come upon him, it passed, and he lowered his eyes to the trail.

Finally, when they had climbed high onto the mountain, Aramus saw that they were emerging onto an icy ledge; a white, frostbitten plateau that led to a brooding black cave. Guarded by dark wolves, the sepulchral entrance was framed by the pale light of night.

Even as Aramus saw the cave he knew that he had seen it before, in his nightmare beside the stream. Unconsciously he halted, staring at the cavern, listening intently to thoughts that promised him failure and pain and persecution beyond all endurance. And as he hesitated, he sensed that his newborn faith, the faith he had gained beside Saul, was nearly exhausted. His fatigue and his pain and the consuming hopelessness of his fears only confirmed what his dark thoughts accused: that here was the end of all hope, the beginning of a suffering he had never known or imagined.

Incomel turned, regarding Aramus and Kaleel with gleaming eyes. A smile twisted the cruel mouth, and the lion looked into the cave, then back again.

"You fear what dwells within?" the creature rasped. "And well you should. For in a moment you will stand living before the throne of Corbis. And then you will die."

Casting a contemptuous smile, the lion turned and walked into the cave. And as if compelled by some dark, supernatural dread, Aramus followed, beside Kaleel, and was swallowed by the grave.

♦ ♦ ♦

Windgate circled the blackened dome of ice, cautiously avoiding the cavern entrance. Moving with long bounds, remaining on hardened ice to avoid tracks, he picked a soundless path along the slope, moving up and down the treacherous incline, searching for what he knew was there.

Following the silver wolf to the mountain had not been easy. Often and with alarming haste he had been forced to find a cunning hiding place to avoid marauding wolves abroad in the land. But he had remained undetected, his long experience and unflinching nerve serving him well.

Only moments before, concealed within a snowy mound near the entrance, he had watched the silver

wolf descend into the pit. And even there he would
follow, if he could only find a way.

But the entrance was too well-guarded. There would
be another way, he knew. And with silent, cautious
movements, he began to circle the mountain's frozen
dome. Yet even as he ascended the slope, ice and sleet
and the howling wind lashed savagely at his frozen fur,
and he began to shiver strongly from the cold.

Descending with crushing strength, the ice storm that
crowned the mountain had suddenly released its full
strength upon him. Shivering, Windgate resisted the
freezing embrace that coated his fur, using the agony of
the killing cold to make himself more determined, more
methodical, in his search. Quickly he moved up the
slope and down, careful to keep his scent from the
cavern entrance. And though he moved with desperate
speed, he still failed to find what he sought.

Jagged lightning blazed across the blackened sky as if
the mountain were angry at his secret approach, and a
hideous rage electrified the air. Windgate sensed the
hellish anger, and he laughed, even as his shivering
increased and the gloom enclosed him in a deathly
shroud. Defiantly he continued his savage hunt, moving
rapidly, relentlessly, using even the brief lightning to spy
out the deep crevices hidden by shadow.

For an eternity, it seemed, he searched and searched
until finally, despite his fierce resolve, Windgate began
to feel a deep exhaustion in his limbs, and his violent
shivering began to slow. Yet he continued to move,
slower now, and with clumsy steps, dimly perceiving that

his thoughts were becoming disjointed and confused, as if his mind were freezing with his blood.

On and on he stumbled, searching across the frozen dome, aware that his once-careful movements were becoming reckless. His efforts seemed suicidal, but somewhere in his frozen mind he knew that if he did not soon find a way into the mountain, he would die on this blackened ice. And as he wearily crossed a sharp ridge, the jagged edge hardened by the killing wind that chilled him deep with cold frost, he found it.

Hidden within the obscure shadow of an icy slab, a darkened pit loomed open and unguarded before him. Windgate smiled at the carelessness, laughing silently into the mist that howled across him. Then he scowled, brown eyes gleaming fiercely as he crept stealthily forward, and was submerged by a darkness beyond anything he had ever known.

seven

Alone in the vast Abyss, Aramus sensed the end of all things. The air was still, but the darkness lived. Thicker, more substantial than darkness, it seemed to ebb and flow, struggling to be unleashed.

Silver eyes adjusting to the thick gloom, Aramus rested on the cold granite floor, every sense alert to detect motion or life in the cavern. A ghastly light, pale and unnatural, hung like frost in the tomblike air, but there was nothing he could see or hear in the shadowy gloom.

Aramus did not know where the wolves had taken Kaleel. He hoped his friend was unharmed, but their separation in the darkness had been so silent and fast that before Aramus realized what had happened, he was standing alone in the cavern. Even Incomel had slid nervously into the shadows.

Aramus felt a soft wind stirring from some unseen corridor, and he sniffed. Strange scents permeated the cavern, making identification difficult, but Aramus found Baalkor's scent, and Incomel's. And other scents were strong, as if the creatures waited, silent and close.

His hopes crushed, Aramus lowered his head, pondering his dark fate, a fate so different from what he had envisioned only days before. After his victorious battle with Baalkor he had dreamed of returning home to a new life, a life of leadership and happiness. Now all his dreams were gone, gone, leaving only memories to ease the loneliness in his soul.

Suddenly an appalling scent emerged from the stygian gloom before him. Instantly, mane bristling, Aramus was on his feet, snarling at the horrifying presence. Prehistoric and primordial, the scent held the taste of something hellishly evil, something that worshiped dead things and feasted on the living.

Even stronger than before, the darkness about Aramus seemed to condense, as if demonic strength were claiming corporeal form, congealing into a burdening mass that weighed down his flesh as closely as horror weighed down his heart. And as the conquering black tide swirled about him, dominating the frosty light, Aramus strained to see the shape that was commanding the Night.

Almost before he realized what he beheld, a faint outline loomed dimly visible before him: a colossal, godlike entity that rested, unmoving, upon a gigantic throne of black granite. Aramus could not comprehend how the massive creature had moved upon him without sound. But it was suddenly there, and it had not been there before. Aramus blinked, focusing, his keen eyes scanning its gigantic girth.

Monstrous and brooding, the entity dissolved into the darkness, blending into the blackness of the cavern, as if it were one with the Abyss. Yet the massive head was visible, outlined by the faint gray light.

Aramus counted the moments with nervous breaths, waiting, and watching, his mind beyond fear as he had known it. Whether the thing was bear or lion or god he did not know, but it was before him. And standing in its unholy presence he felt an awesome and unreal power, as if he stood before the full scope of created might, the end of all strength.

Mountainously, rumbling with brute, beastly power, the colossus shifted. A cavernous breath sighed into the tomblike air, weary and aged. And Aramus knew that he stood before Corbis, chief of the Dark Council.

"You bleed," a ponderous voice echoed in the Abyss.

Aramus waited, silent.

"So . . ." it whispered. "You are the son of Gianavel."

Aramus struggled to speak.

"I am the son of Gianavel," he said quietly. "And like my father, I defy you."

Corbis's thunderous laugh blasted past him, hot with hate.

"Defy me?" the voice continued, amused. "A wolf cub defies me?"

Aramus did not know how to reply. Vaguely, he expected to be struck down by the Beast. But Corbis only laughed.

"And what do you defy?" the Beast said softly.

Aramus stared, confused.

"Do you think darkness dwells only within the Abyss?" the voice whispered. "No, young cub. The darkness that embraces you, even now, is only the darkness of your heart. Yes, listen closely, and you'll know my words are true. You alone know your own lusts, your failures, your secret desires. But you know that they rule your heart. For how often have you enjoyed those hidden pleasures, young cub? How often have you turned your back on what you knew was right? Yes, many, many times. I know you. I know you, even as I know myself. How often have you embraced evil when you could have chosen good? Is that not the darkness of your heart?"

A rumbling laugh shook the cavern.

"Behold . . . the darkness of your heart."

Aramus opened his mouth to speak, but his thoughts were instantly submerged beneath a swirling darkness that burst forth from the cavern and into his mind, drowning his thoughts beneath a cascade of accusing voices, condemning him for every failure, every evil desire, conceived or imagined, and every careless word. For a moment Aramus resisted, but the attack was overwhelming, its strength beyond the strength of flesh to endure.

Corbis continued, commanding and unrelenting.

"Yes, behold, young cub. Darkness shall always win in the end. There is no power that can defy the Dark Lord. But still you refuse, don't you? Yes, I sense your spirit resisting the Dark Lord's might. Then listen to your heart, and it shall teach you. For darkness is the first power, and the last. It has always ruled your heart, and always shall. Nothing can resist."

Silver eyes focused fiercely upon the Beast.

"Saul . . . resisted," Aramus whispered. "He never . . . surrendered."

Corbis seemed moved by the quiet words. And Aramus felt, even through the darkness, an immense power suddenly stir within the colossus; something cosmic, infinite and irresistible.

"Yes . . . the great Saul," Corbis muttered, a hated remembrance echoing in the words. "And tell me, where is the great Saul now? He is dead, destroyed by his own stupidity and cut to pieces while he lived! Don't be a fool, young cub, as he was. Serve me! Cease this foolish resistance!"

Aramus stared fully into the hated glare.

"I will serve . . . the Lightmaker," he whispered, but felt his strength crumbling under the long physical strain of his ordeal. "My life is with him. You have . . . no real power."

"Power?" Corbis laughed, hateful and cold. "Behold . . . power!"

Suddenly memories long dead and long buried were resurrected together, reminding Aramus of all he had ever loved, and lost. Aramus closed his eyes against the pain, lowering his head, groaning with wounds that cut deeper than fang ever could. He shook his head, trying to throw off the true horrors of his life. But when he concentrated, his thoughts were like nothing at all. Corbis laughed again, invading his mind with the sadistic mirth. Aramus felt as if he stood alone, in space, with only the Beast before him.

"I . . . still . . . resist you," Aramus said softly, though his voice sounded muffled and indistinct.

"Then you must understand . . . what you resist," whispered the Beast. And the wolf's silver mane shivered, as if from a dark wind.

Submerged within the hideousness of its hate, Aramus sensed a vision rising before him, a vision of a wide, expansive darkness that unfolded, crushing the cold earth beneath a merciless wrath. And all flesh was cast down together beneath the darkness. And the night was filled with hopeless cries and hopeless prayers, each voice a merciful plea, but only darkness answered. Aramus saw the darkness sweep across the earth, echoing with shrieks of pain, and suffering, and pain again. And all the living beheld one another in their fear, saw the hopelessness of their lives, and there was horror and madness and death. Yet there was no war, for life and death and treasures together had become meaningless beneath the domination of night. And those who were still living looked upon each other with faces of flame, amazed at the terror that had befallen them, while suffering winds swept barren beneath the moonless sky, bearing nothing with the pale air but the

doom of lost and lonely souls, alone in the endless void.
And on and on the darkness swept, as day and light
were forgotten, defeated by the power of Night that
slowed the earth, slowed it, until all that was, was no
more.

"So... now you know," Corbis's voice echoed in the
stillness. "And do you still resist that force which shall
be the end of all things? Or will you rule beside me in
the world to come? What shall it be, young cub? Shall it
be life? Or shall it be death?"

Aramus's thoughts were lost beneath the darkness
sweeping across his mind. So confused, so defeated was
he that he could not remember a time when he had
been victorious over his fears. This conflict was beyond
him, beyond his strength, beyond his years, beyond all
the wisdom and knowledge he possessed. He opened his
mouth to speak, and realized he was only staring vacantly at Corbis. Yet, with a trembling effort, Aramus
managed a word, hardly remembering the question but
knowing that his answer must be somehow defiant.

"Death," he said weakly.

Corbis glowered upon him, the brooding frown
casting a cold presence across the cavern.

"So shall it be," came the godlike whisper. "Yet I will
not stir my strength to destroy you. When Baalkor
returns from the border of your mountain home, he shall
spill your blood in the Abyss."

Then Corbis laughed, and guards, menacing wolves of
fearsome size, suddenly appeared beside Aramus. He
knew they were there, but was too exhausted to care,

and failed to fight as they led him from the chamber and into the darkness beyond.

◆ ◆ ◆

Even as the silver wolf disappeared into the depths of the granite corridor, Incomel stood before the throne of Corbis. The lion's eyes glimmered menacingly in the gloom, and though the proud voice was angry, it re-tained a wide edge of respect, and fear.

"Is this wise, great Corbis?" Incomel growled. "You know the child's father will come for him. Even here," the lion raised its head, gesturing to the Abyss, "the father will come for him."

Corbis's roaring laugh boomed through the shadows that cloaked the demonic domain. And the laugh roared on and on, trembling the tomb, until at last the walls echoed cavernously with some unspeakable delight, some incomprehensible evil.

"Do you think there is anything my vast intellect has not considered, Incomel?" Corbis laughed. "There is no thought hidden from my sight. I know Gianavel will come for his son. That is the reason he is here."

Incomel's words were hard with hate.

"Do not forget, Corbis. The father is not the son. I have fought Gianavel before. His invincible mind cannot be shaken, nor can his faith be broken. I tell you the truth. The old wolf is dangerous."

Corbis's penetrating, probing gaze studied the lion.

"You fear the wolf."

Incomel's proud gaze did not waver.

"I fear nothing," he replied.

Corbis was silent, brooding, the sadistic eyes gazing into another world, another dimension, where some ancient, malevolent entity heard and responded to his unearthly thoughts. And as the moments passed, the eyes glared, mesmerized, as if beholding an insidious, corrupting force that spoke hotly to his heart.

"No," whispered Corbis, frowning, his vacant stare focused on that unseen darkness. "You do not fear Gianavel. It is the spirit within him that you fear."

Incomel's face was grim.

"God walks with the old wolf, Corbis," he said bitterly. "Many have tried to destroy Gianavel, and their bones are scattered in the hills. Gianavel is old, but he is strong in his age. Even in war he does not forget wisdom, but always finds an advantage. And his strength goes beyond flesh. The Lightmaker has never allowed anyone to defeat him in battle."

Corbis smiled from his throne of darkness, and once again focused fully on the lion.

"Do not fear the wolf, great Incomel. The Dark Lord is stronger than the Lightmaker. Even now, though we have not yet assembled all the power of the cosmos, our strength is sufficient for the task. Only the old wolf stands in our way."

Magnetic and hypnotic, Corbis's eyes gleamed as he leaned forward.

"Strike down Gianavel and the Lightmaker's servants will be scattered. And for this great service to the Dark

Lord you will be granted a great reward. You will ascend in strength beyond your glorified state to become as I am, with knowledge of all things. There will be no secret pleasure, no delight, hidden from your eyes. Yet your victory shall not end there. No, for when Gianavel is destroyed, the last, great servant of the Lightmaker shall be gone. Then all faith will be shattered, and the power will return to the cosmos, where it will be absorbed by the Dark Lord, who will deliver it unto me. And we shall pass beyond time, beyond life, beyond death. We shall rule all that was, or is, or is to come. We will ascend beyond these mortal tombs of flesh and bone, becoming what we were truly meant to be: gods on the Earth."

Only a moment did the lion hesitate, demonic eyes glowering with some consuming, cosmic lust, some ancient hunger. And from somewhere within the great black form, an insatiable and imperious ambition seemed to emerge, destroying everything but its own commanding desire to consume more, to possess more, to know no limitations but its own. Then Incomel turned, irresistible strength moving with effortless grace, and was absorbed by the darkness.

eight

Aramus was dead, as dead as he could be and yet live. He lay with head down and eyes closed, hoping to find sleep to ease his pain, but his mind was troubled and distracted, and sleep escaped his grasp.

By what incomprehensible force Corbis had summoned his hellish powers, he did not know, but the Beast's overpowering presence had smashed his mind to pieces with its relentless attack. Aramus shook his head, trying to clear his thoughts, but they remained confused and clouded.

Aramus realized that Baalkor's demonic influence was nothing compared to the irresistible strength of Corbis. And now, after being shamed and conquered by the cruel force of that strength, Aramus felt as if his visions, his dreams, were gone, destroyed forever by the

conquering black mist that had overwhelmed his heart and soul.

He lifted his eyes to the walls of his cell, searching for the strength that had sustained him beside Saul. Somewhere within his heart he felt his spirit stir with the effort, but his soul was wasted, wearied beyond the place where he could stand alone.

Within him his suffering seemed like living flames consuming his mind and heart. And slowly, as the painful moments passed, Aramus felt a burning suffering that embraced all that he was. He stared vacantly at the rough walls, lost to his suffering, lost to his pain. And still the flames increased, building within his heart until the flames became a blaze, and the blaze flamed into an inferno that filled him, filled him, driving out everything from within him but the consuming pain of his suffering. Aramus felt his heart break at the pain, and his heart reached out. And suddenly he was lying again with Saul, together in the snow, and the old hare was speaking to his heart . . .

"*His grace is sufficient . . . his grace is sufficient . . . always strength comes for the task. . . .*"

Aramus laughed, even as the tears formed and the flames continued, annihilating his hopes in the holocaust of his pain. Yet even as his dreams died and his heart was consumed with his pain, Aramus began to gain a deeper understanding, an understanding that revealed all the true and final motivations of his heart. Enduring his pain, Aramus watched as all that he had ever cherished above the Lightmaker was engulfed by

those relentless flames, the holocaust that spared
nothing in his heart. And as he watched the death of
his deepest desires, Aramus sensed the spirit of the
Lightmaker rising strongly within him, but that spirit
only increased the fury of the flames even more, utterly
destroying within him what could never have been
destroyed by any less a force.

"Always strength comes for the task. . . ."

Then, as Aramus watched, the spirit of the Lightmaker slowly took what the holocaust had destroyed,
gathering the shattered remnants of his life and
recreating them again with a purer purpose, reforging his
heart and soul into something more than he had ever
been, something bold and unyielding and strong with
ancient strength, something he had never imagined and
never conceived that he could be—the image of his
Father.

Aramus breathed softly with the spirit that continued
to rise within him. And as the spirit increased, his heart
grew calm and his thoughts cleared. And the spirit
revealed to him his mind, his hidden thoughts and fears,
and with amazing clarity Aramus suddenly understood
his illusions, and the reasons for his fears. Even in his
fatigue, Aramus was amazed at the clearness of his
understanding, and wondered why he had never
understood before. For it seemed as if he had known the
truth all his life, yet without knowing. And as he
continued to seek the Lightmaker through his pain, he
sensed a new strength, knowing that never again would
illusions and fear have dominion over him; for his mind

had been set free, the power of lies destroyed at last by the spirit that had lifted the death shroud from his eyes.

Aramus realized that if he survived this struggle, he would never again look at life in the same way. Never again would he find consolation in circumstances, knowing that circumstances could change. And never again would he feel defeat in suffering, knowing that suffering, however great, could be endured and would only temper him for a harder design, enabling his heart and mind to endure what could not have been endured before.

"Always strength comes. . . ."

Sadness faded, replaced by a deepening peace, and Aramus finally rested, smiling faintly, knowing that now, indeed, an awesome strength, hard-gained and long-awaited, had come for the task.

Lost in his communion with that sacred spirit within him, Aramus almost missed the small eyes staring excitedly at him from the entrance of the cell. Then, sensing the creature's presence, he looked up sharply, alert to attack.

Instantly Aramus was on his feet, for he recognized the dark outline in the doorway. It was the hare from Saul's colony, the one who had spotted him across the field near the southern caves.

Brown eyes flashing nervously, the big hare stared in wonder as the silver wolf loomed over it. Its powerfully muscled legs jerked twice as if suppressing a desire to flee, but it did not move. Aramus saw its fear, and he spoke quietly, soothingly. He did not think of attack, for no longer did he choose friend or foe by nature, but by the spirit within them. And he knew that the hare was a servant of the Lightmaker, as Saul before him.

"What are you doing here?" Aramus whispered.

A nervous voice replied.

"I am Windgate, now king of the Colony near the Deep Woods. And I am here to help you. I know that, somehow, you stood beside my king, Saul. And debt for debt, I will repay."

So quietly, so quickly did the hare whisper the fierce words that Aramus was spellbound. Briefly, the big hare's presence returned Aramus to that stormy night in the glade, when Baalkor had made him fight for what he believed. And he remembered Saul's dying words, "but for brave Windgate... we would have been destroyed."

Aramus focused on the hare, so fierce, so brave, so loyal to his departed king.

"I am Aramus, son of Gianavel," he said. "And it is true, Saul and I stood together. He was my friend, and he spoke of you. But," he added, looking over the hare's shoulder, fearing the approach of a random patrol, "you are in great danger. How did you get in here? How did you find me?"

Windgate was quickly recovering from his initial nervousness, and his eyes gleamed with excitement.

"There is a way that is unguarded!" he whispered fiercely. "Saul would not have made such a mistake! Hurry, we'll escape while it's still dark. We'll outrun them in the forest. But there's no time to waste!"

Aramus thrilled with sudden hope. And for a tense, tempting moment he glared excitedly down the corridor, anxious to escape. Then he remembered Kaleel, and he sighed, shaking his head wearily.

"No. You must go," he said. "I don't know where they've taken the bear, Kaleel. And he is my friend. I won't leave him alone."

Windgate's eyes blazed. "We can find him, too! Let's get out of here!"

Aramus weighed the risk. Could they search the corridors until they found Kaleel, and still fight their way out? He considered a long moment. No, he thought, it would be impossible. Incomel was too powerful to fight. And countless guards were constantly patrolling the passages of the Abyss. Aramus could not even imagine how the brave hare had managed to penetrate the defense. He shook his head again.

"No. We'll never be able to find Kaleel without them finding us first. There are too many halls, too many cells to search. How did you manage to reach me? Guards are everywhere."

Windgate sniffed contemptuously.

"Idiots!" he said. "I've seen snails with more brains. I've roamed up and down these corridors, crawling behind their backs, and they still haven't seen me. They're arrogant and proud. Saul was right. Their pride will be their downfall."

Aramus almost laughed, joyous to see the big hare so defiant, before the urgency of Windgate's peril returned to him. Every moment the hare remained increased his chances for discovery and instant death.

"I'm not leaving Kaleel," Aramus said quietly. "You're brave, but there's nothing else you can do here. Baalkor will be returning soon and—"

"Baalkor?" snarled Windgate. "He is the one?"

Aramus looked at the hare, nodded tersely.

Windgate's eyes narrowed, unbelievably menacing for one so small.

"May the Lightmaker destroy him for what he has done!" His words were hard with wrath. "But if you will not go with me, then perhaps there is another way I can serve you. I know something that you don't know. I saw you in the big room when you spoke with the fat one."

Aramus blinked, considering.

"Corbis?"

"Yes, the fat one," said Windgate. "And I heard him speak with the lion after they took you away. They don't want you. They want your father. I heard them speak of him. That is why they brought you here. They want to lure your father down from the North so they can kill him. Even now the lion is hunting him on the mountain. They know that your father will come for you."

Aramus closed his eyes.

"My father," he whispered, silver brow furrowed. He lowered his head for a moment, grieved at Windgate's words.

"I will find your father!" said the big hare fiercely. "I will warn him about their trap! And I will show him the hidden entrance. He will know what to do."

Aramus felt his hopes revive with the desperate plan. But could Windgate find Gianavel in that vast wilderness? Aramus knew how cunning and elusive his father could be. He thought furiously and remembered the black ledge that bordered the trail leading up the mountain.

"You'll never find my father in the forest," he said. "But neither will they. He's too smart and too fast. Nothing will stop him from reaching the mountain. If you go out looking for him, you won't see him. You must wait for him to come to you. That's the only way to get near him. Now, listen, there's not much time," he cautioned. "There's only one way up the mountain, and that's the trail we followed to the cave. Do you remember the small plateau about halfway up the path, the one that looks down on the trail?"

Windgate nodded tensely.

"That's where you'll have to wait. My father will climb the trail. There's no other way up the mountain. And if you wait for him on the plateau, he'll pass right beneath you. But you'll have to watch closely because he won't make a sound and he'll be moving at night."

Aramus looked down the corridor again, watching for the guards. Nervously he weighed the hare's impossible task. It would be difficult to descend the mountain undetected, even to the ledge. And Aramus knew that his father would be hard to locate in the darkness,

concealed within his great stealth. And even if Windgate did find his father, how would a warning save the
old wolf from Incomel? With a sense of rising dread
Aramus remembered the lion's matchless speed and
strength. How could his father defeat it? But he could
think of nothing else to do.

He turned his attention to Windgate again and saw
the hare studying him intently.

"Your wounds are not serious," Windgate said, looking
closely at the talon marks. "You'll survive."

"I know, my friend," said Aramus. "But now you must
leave. Quickly. You have to find my father."

Aramus hesitated, thinking furiously.

"But my father is suspicious, always careful, especially
in times of war. He may not trust you. If he doubts, tell
him, 'Aramus said: be strong, be courageous, do what
you know is right,' and he'll know I sent you. Now, go.
Tell my father that Incomel is hunting him."

Windgate's eyes glinted hard for a moment, and the
hare's voice was harsh and tense.

"I shall not fail you," he said, smiling fiercely. And
with that his dark eyes gleamed, as if he found pleasure
in defying these massive beasts and the evil god they
served. Then, with only the slightest scurry of padded
feet, he bounded away down the corridor.

◆　◆　◆

Moving in the very shadow of the mountain,
Gianavel found a perilous path through the night. He
was close now, he knew, and he could sense the danger.

Wary of a trap, the old wolf constantly scanned the darkness, searching for shadows that moved, but he saw nothing. And careful to conceal his outline within the trees that fringed the mountain, he continued slowly forward, never venturing across the open slope lest the light of the moon reveal his lonely shape.

Patiently, patiently, Gianavel found a silent path, avoiding twigs and rocks, moving with infinite grace and infinite skill, always searching, relentlessly alert for a guard. But there was nothing, only shades of black and gray in the gloom.

Gianavel followed the haggard stand of trees as it curved away from the path. He could move more quickly if he remained on the trail that tracked out across the shattered ridge before him. But the treeline would cross the path again on the other side of the slope. And he would have to avoid detection to reach his son. He was too close to the Abyss to survive a physical conflict in the open ground.

So quiet, so subdued, was the mountain that Gianavel felt compelled to forsake caution for speed. Yet he controlled his desire for haste, moving with disciplined steps along his careful path. And whether it was sound or scent or something half-sensed, Gianavel would never know, but a deadly thrill suddenly alerted him to a threatening presence traveling through the darkness along the ridge.

Even as he felt the presence Gianavel's great gray form froze, unmoving in the night, one foot held aloft. Still as stone, the old wolf listened intently, searching every whisper for what had alerted him, but he recognized nothing. He stood listening, listening, but only the wind whispered in the night. And Gianavel began to fear that whatever he had sensed might also have sensed him.

Slowly, without moving his gray head, Gianavel turned his eyes to look cautiously at the darkened hillside. He stared intensely at the ridge, seeing nothing. Yet still he did not move, knowing that his senses had not betrayed him. Something he could not identify had alerted him to a hidden danger, so he stood silently and waited. And with acute skill he searched the wind, but the air was still, deathly still, as if it, too, were afraid to move.

Suddenly, hideously, Gianavel sensed a demonic power reaching out for him, searching the night, a power he had known before. And he was certain that the unseen beast, too, had felt him traveling through the darkness. Without movement or sound, Gianavel suppressed a snarl. He had no wish to fight, no wish to kill, but fight and kill he would to save his son. Silently, the old wolf stood, hidden within the shadow of an ancient elm. And as the long moments passed he prayed, asking the Lightmaker to conceal his presence.

A long time the old wolf stood, acutely searching the source of every whispered sound, his heart beating heavily in his massive chest. His breathing grew strained and tense, but still he did not turn his shaggy gray head for a better look at the darkened ridge. He knew that patience and discipline would determine the victor of this battle.

Then, as if a living shadow had separated from the darkness, Gianavel suddenly saw a faint movement. Quickly he focused on the shape, previously obscured within the greater gloom of the hillside, and it rapidly grew clearer. The old wolf read every shade, every pattern of darkness surrounding the shape. And as the moments passed he began to recognize the dim outline of a great, lionlike beast standing silently on the slope. Though the beast was partially hidden by boulders and shattered rock, Gianavel recognized its dark aspect. And he knew that if Incomel had not made the mistake of moving, he would never have seen it at all.

Ages, it seemed, the lion stood upon the hill, motionless again in the darkness. And it stood for so long that, had Gianavel not already felt its hideous strength, he would have doubted that he had truly seen the slight movement. He would have doubted that the shadow had ever shifted, would have suspected that it had all been a trick of his tired eyes. But the great wolf knew in his heart that the lion was there. It had made one mistake. But it was enough.

Long years of hard discipline gave Gianavel the edge, allowing him to remain still, his breath so hushed, so shallow, that not even his acute ears could detect any sound. And finally, after an eternity of watchful tension, the lion turned soundlessly on the hillside, moving away, and vanished over the ridge.

Yet, still, Gianavel did not react. Endlessly patient, he stood in the night, attempting to detect another unseen presence, wary of a trap. His gray eyes searched the shadows with intensified alertness, leaving nothing unexplored.

Only after his cautious wisdom was satisfied did the old wolf finally move again, stepping in absolute silence, a gray ghost that defied the dead, conquering demons and flesh together with his spirit and skill.

n i n e

Cunningly concealed beneath a slab of black ice, Windgate waited, and watched, as a pale dawn rose above the mountain, casting a slight hue through the storm clouds.

Breathing hard, he gathered his strength, recovering from the ordeal of descending the path from the Abyss. For only by the boldest of risks had he narrowly avoided two wolf packs, once desperately throwing himself beneath a sheet of dark ice that rested on the trail itself, so that the wolves almost stepped upon his still form. How the dark sentinels missed his scent, Windgate would never know, but they had passed over him in ignorance as he lay, shivering, underneath the ice. Nervous and exhausted, anticipating at any moment a fatal attack, he had finally reached the plateau as the last stars vanished from the night sky.

And now he waited, patiently and silently, for
another nightfall, knowing that Gianavel would not
come up the path in the revealing light of day. He
shifted beneath the cold concealment, fighting off the
chill that crept upon him from the blackened ice, and
wondered how long he could last before his senses were
numbed by the merciless cold. He glanced up at the
dark clouds encircling the mountain, crowning the
glacier in a storm of lightning and snow and ice. And he
frowned, despising their strength. Then he looked back
to the trail beneath him.

Fighting off sleep, Windgate struggled to remain alert,
knowing that his scent and tracks still marked his path
to the plateau. Eventually, he knew, he would be discovered. And as the thought came upon him, he looked
back over his shoulder at his escape route.

A narrow ledge, treacherous and glazed with ice,
began behind him, running alongside a sheer cliff that
bordered a gaping chasm. Windgate had carefully studied
the ledge after he had arrived, calculating that he could
negotiate the path safely enough, though any creature of
size would be hard put to pursue. On impulse, the big
hare glanced into the chasm, deep and frightening and
heavy with snow. And he smiled, laughing silently. He
would like to see a wolf follow him over that.

The trio of dark wolves were beneath him almost
before Windgate heard their muffled steps. Cautiously,
he peered down upon the trail from the shadow of his
icy lair.

The wolves were studying the tiny tracks that ran up the slope to his place of hiding. Dark eyes peered suspiciously upward as they searched along the plateau.

Windgate did not move. He knew that, even though he was hidden well within the shadows, any sudden movement would reveal his presence. Motionless, as motionless as the shadows that shrouded him, he waited, and stared back.

Below, the dark muscular forms tensed, as if debating whether to explore the curious tracks or resume their patrol. Windgate watched their deliberation in strained silence, knowing that, while difficult, it would not be impossible for a wolf to pursue him along his escape route. And as the moments passed, he unconsciously scowled at the beasts, beginning to hope that they would, indeed, pursue him along the narrow trail. For with cunning and courage, he might take one of them with him over the edge. He smiled grimly. Death would be sweet in such a bitter embrace.

Finally, the sentries began to slowly climb the narrow slope, following the trampled snow to discover the cause of the curious tracks.

Moving with experienced stealth, Windgate eased backwards from beneath the blackened slab until he stood unseen on the plateau. Then he bounded quickly and quietly to the chasm, its icy depths hidden beneath clouds, and leaped onto the ledge.

So narrowly and slenderly did the ledge slant away from the slope that Windgate had trouble maintaining balance. But he knew he had only moments before the

wolves emerged upon the plateau and saw his fleeing
form, so he raced down the edge, intent on rounding a
bend in the chasm wall before they saw him. If they did
not observe his retreat, they might be more reluctant to
pursue.

Concentrating, he bounded along the ledge through
the first sharp bend, hoping that the slender path might
eventually widen, allowing secure purchase. But as he
passed the curve, he saw that the trail only twisted on
and on along the darkened wall, narrow and treacherous
and broken.

He stopped and waited on the far side of the wall,
listening to the wolves as they reached the plateau and
began pacing near the ledge, knowing his direction but
hesitant to pursue along the treacherous path. He
laughed silently, feeling safe once again. He would rest
here until they decided to return to their patrol. Then
he would resume his watch for Gianavel.

As Windgate waited, he looked out across the chasm,
studying the relentless ice walls, cold and cruel and
conquering, and he was strangely awed by the desolation, and saddened by the depth of the power before
him. For it seemed, in the timeless solitude of the
moment, that nothing could resist such cruelty, such
ageless might. At once and in total, Windgate thought
he perceived the true scope of the Dark Lord's wrath.
And for one brief moment, as he stood alone and cold
and isolated on that perilous edge of the void, he feared
that perhaps, indeed, the forces of darkness would prove
stronger in the end.

Then, almost with thought, a resolute spirit flooded through him, strengthening him with that mysterious power that always enabled him to stand firm when his flesh was afraid. Windgate had never really understood that unknown power, how it encouraged him or what awakened its strength. But he knew that it was the Lightmaker's touch. And, still, after all these years, he was amazed at how that spirit caused him to stand when his knees trembled.

He turned, intending to chance a quick look at the plateau, when he spotted a narrow crevice behind him, all but concealed by overhanging ice. Alarmed that he had not noticed the cleft earlier, he studied the opening suspiciously.

Narrow and ominous, the slender cleft was slashed viciously with ice. And as he looked closer, Windgate realized that he had not earlier seen the narrow opening because it was hidden well behind an outcropping of black rock.

Carefully, Windgate crept forward, strangely frightened but intrigued by the cave. He knew that it would be a good hiding place. For even if the dark wolves found the courage to pursue him along the ledge, they would not likely come this far. And if they chanced a cautious look around the bend, they would still not see this place of concealment, hidden from that direction by ice and rock. They would see only the narrow trail running endlessly and dangerously along the chasm wall.

Wasting no time once his decision was made, Windgate leapt through the narrow entrance and

turned, positioning himself to evade the chilling wind.
Almost as soon as he was inside the cavern, a wave of
contentment swept over his frosted form, making him
feel suddenly warmer, safer. Quietly and comfortably he
rested, enjoying his satisfaction in having escaped the
cold wind and the wolves with his daring move.

It was a long time before he felt, with a sudden thrill
of fear, the stare that rested on his back. And then a
wolf scent reached him, so real and so close that he
almost leapt, livid with fear, back upon the ledge. But
even as he knew the scent, Windgate realized that
something was strangely wrong or he would have already
been attacked.

Slowly, eyes moving far ahead of his stiffening flesh,
Windgate turned, searching, dreading what he might
find. And behind him, standing silently in the gloom of
the icy cavern, he saw it.

Gigantic and majestic, the gray wolf stood in the
darkness, motionless as the granite walls. Its massive
form struck Windgate with both fear and relief, for even
in the shadows he knew the symmetry of that powerful
frame, recognizing instantly the father from the son.

Yet, as Windgate looked more closely, the old wolf
seemed somehow weary, haggard, the stern face drawn,
as if from the ordeal of a long and difficult journey. And
the gray coat was ragged, windblown, and torn with
thorns.

Carefully, Windgate turned to face the great wolf,
who watched him through veiled eyes. No trace of
emotion or threat was visible in that gray visage, and

Windgate knew that here was a creature who, dangerous though he could be, bore no ill will toward the world. Then, with cautious steps, Windgate approached the great form, and the stern gray head bowed, respectful and kind.

Windgate's words trembled as he spoke.

"I am Windgate, king of the Colony near the Deep Woods," he whispered. "And I bear words for Gianavel . . . from his son."

Windgate felt as if the old wolf had instantly moved closer, even though he knew it had remained still. The gray eyes narrowed, seeming to know far more than they revealed. Then the kingly face smiled down upon him.

"I am Gianavel."

t e n

Strange days," Windgate whispered. "I would never have found you if the Lightmaker had not led me to this crevice. I have been waiting and watching for you to approach the mountain. I didn't think you would already be upon the ice."

"I came upon the ledge last night," the great wolf said quietly. "I know that I am close to the Abyss. I have been here before."

Windgate glanced over his shoulder at the narrow, icy ledge and wondered at the dauntless courage that had enabled the great wolf to hazard that treacherous trail, hampered by darkness. Yet Gianavel seemed to think nothing of the task, his stern visage despising the challenge of the ice and ledge and mountain together. His gray eyes gazed down, commanding and inspiring.

"And what do you know of my son?" Gianavel asked.

Even standing in the presence of this natural enemy, Windgate sensed no danger. Rather, he felt accepted and shielded by the power of the great wolf, embraced by the warmth of its spirit and strengthened by its majestic presence.

"He is a prisoner in the Abyss," Windgate said, his words spilling out rapidly, "but I have found a secret entrance, a way that is unguarded! But Aramus would not leave without another who is being held there. Kaleel, the bear."

Gianavel nodded solemnly, as if confirming what he had long suspected.

"Aramus has befriended the bear," he said. "I perceived as much. I have followed their scent together since their first battle on the ridge. But how is my child? How badly is he hurt? I know he fought with Incomel in the forest."

"His wounds are not great," said Windgate. "He will survive. But he says that Baalkor is to kill him when he returns. I tried to get him to come with me, but he wouldn't leave Kaleel. So he sent me to warn you. This is a trap. Corbis does not care about Aramus. Corbis wants you. All this has been a trick to lure you here. I overheard Corbis when he was talking with Incomel. The lion is supposed to hunt you down. They know you are going to come for Aramus. Incomel is hunting you, even now."

Gianavel shook his head.

"Incomel will hunt for me only at night, hoping the darkness will give him the power he needs to overcome me. We have many hours of daylight remaining, so we don't have to worry about him until then. He will stay within the Abyss during the light."

Windgate scowled, considering.

"But he fought with Aramus in the light," he said.

"He was not afraid of Aramus," said Gianavel, simply. "Now, tell me, where are they keeping my son, and where is the bear?"

"I couldn't find the bear. But Aramus is not far from the throne of Corbis. There are guards everywhere. It is no easy thing to get close to him. But I know the way! We can go there now!"

Gianavel shook his head.

"No. Not now. Incomel remains within the Abyss. If we are discovered, with the lion inside the cave, we will not survive the fight. My pack is coming. Today, or tonight at the latest. Then we will have strength on our side. Did you say that Baalkor returns soon?"

"Yes. Perhaps tonight."

"Then we'll wait until tonight. And if Baalkor returns early, then we must attack early, without the pack."

Gianavel paused, seeming to debate within himself.

"I perceive that doom is upon the Dark Council. And I have sensed that the Lightmaker will destroy them before this fight is finished. But we must do all that flesh can do. We can't do anything about Corbis. He will not come out of the Abyss. And Baalkor isn't here, so we can't do anything about him. Incomel, alone, remains. If the lion is gone, then our chances of victory will be greater."

Gianavel gazed quietly at Windgate, as if measuring the hare's resolve.

"It seems that it's come down to the two of us," the old wolf said softly. "Will you stand beside me to destroy the beast?"

Windgate nodded fiercely.

"Your spirit is great," Gianavel smiled. "Saul would have been proud."

"You knew Saul?" Windgate asked, his voice sharp with surprise.

"I did," said Gianavel, eyes touched with memory. "I saw him battle Baalkor beside my son."

Windgate's dark eyes softened. "Saul was great."

Gianavel nodded.

"Saul was great, it's true. But so are you, my friend. And the Lightmaker will use your courage for a purpose. We will strike tonight, when Incomel comes forth from the Abyss. If we succeed, the lion will be gone. Then only the power of Corbis and Baalkor will remain. And we'll deal with them when the moment arrives."

Windgate considered the old wolf's words.

"It will not be easy," the hare said. "I have seen the lion fight. He is strong, and fast."

"I know," said Gianavel. "I have fought him before. But he is flesh, and he can be destroyed. Just as Corbis, despite his demonic power, is flesh. They will both fall. Only remember that when the battle becomes fierce we must not flinch from the fight. We must not allow fear to make us weak, or we will surely die. We will get no second chance against the lion. We must be perfect in our cunning, perfect in our attack. We must move with courage and determination, and strike with skill. And after we have done all that flesh can do, the Lightmaker will do the rest."

"How will we destroy him?" Windgate asked, eyes flashing with excitement, charged for the fight.

Gianavel smiled at the dauntless hare, then turned, staring out the entrance of the cavern. And as the moments passed, Windgate sensed a devastating power awakening within the old wolf, an unearthly strength not stirred or conceived by mortal rage, but unleashed by the spirit within. Silent in a silence more terrible than any roar, Gianavel studied the ledge. And the gray eyes narrowed, measuring.

"We'll give him what he wants."

eleven

Concealed again beneath blackened ice, Windgate adamantly resisted the penetrating cold. He had lain all day, until the wintry sun began to descend upon the distant hills, and now the gray evening was upon him. *Not much longer,* Windgate whispered to himself, shivering against the shadowy chill.

Sleepy, fighting off the urge to doze in the cradling snow, Windgate continued his silent vigil until dusky shadows shrouded the mountain, cloaking black granite and dark ice together with the conquering power of night. Steadfast and enduring, Windgate maintained his watch, waiting, waiting for the one he knew would come down the mountain trail, emerging with the darkness to hunt beneath the haunting moon. And it would be then that Windgate would make his desperate move.

A long time he waited, patient and alert, as the
moments crept by in heavy silence. And slowly he began
to fear that perhaps the lion had already come down the
mountain and passed him unseen, concealed within its
demonic power. Windgate shook his head, angry at the
thought, and focused his keen eyes on the dim trail
below him. *The Lightmaker will provide a means of
victory*, he told himself, and concentrated on the
shadows. And finally, after a time, a faint, ghostly
outline moved in the night haze far up the trail, making
no sound, gliding with supernatural grace over the
shattered stone, descending.

Dark and massive, the lion came down the path, its
gigantic frame even more terrifying in the aspect of
night. And as the beast descended, the image of
irresistible strength, Windgate stood, silent and
challenging, upon the cliff edge.

Almost before Windgate had moved, the lion reacted,
dropping into a crouch, a feral snarl exposing gaping
fangs. The hare was struck by a wave of icy fear at the
sight, and suddenly realized that this would be a true test
of nerve. Quickly he asked for the strength, the will, to
honor the Lightmaker with his life, or his death.

Incomel's hateful eyes focused hard, and Windgate felt
an incarnate power sweep over him, as if the mountain
lion had reached out and struck him with the power of
its infernal soul. But the hare did not move, remaining
resolute and defiant, staring down at the beast with
implacable eyes.

For a flashing instant Incomel's suspicious gaze
scanned the rest of the darkened rim, almost as if he
had been nervously prepared for an ambush, ready to
meet some long-dreaded attack. A scowl turned the
corners of Windgate's mouth as he considered the trap
they had laid for the beast. The lion had good reason to
be afraid.

And yet the growl that trembled the cliff face revealed no trace of terror. Undaunted, Windgate smiled
down at the lion and cast his words with contempt.

"Doom is upon you, Incomel!" he shouted. "I am
Windgate, king of the Colony near the Deep Woods, a
servant of the Lightmaker. I challenge you!"

Exploding in a sweeping rush up the mountainside,
the lion closed the distance between them with blinding
speed. And though Windgate had seen Incomel fight
before, he had not anticipated such awesome, unnatural
power and strength. The lion was halfway up the cliff
before Windgate could even react, its devastating roar
ascending before it.

And then Windgate moved, with a blinding spin and
a rush along the plateau, leaping with all the strength of
his powerful legs for the treacherous safety of the narrow
ledge. But even as he rushed forward, the lion roared
over the cliff edge, having cleared the steep face in rapid
bounds.

Overcome by the beast's surpassing speed, Windgate
leapt frantically for the thin ledge. And as he neared his
escape route, another thunderous roar shattered the ice
of the plateau and Windgate felt the hot breath of the

lion upon him. Then the big hare recklessly threw himself upon the narrow edge of the icy ledge, spinning and grasping wildly as he slid toward the chasm. For a moment he swung along the very edge of the precipice, then struck a slice of ice and was looking down on a sea of white clouds. Windgate bellowed, wildly struck something unknown, and was spun back around to dig desperate claws into the black ice.

Breathing hard, unable to speak, unable to think, Windgate tried to recover his racing heart, balancing himself precariously on the unforgiving ice. And after an instant, when his throat had cleared to breathe, he looked wide-eyed at Incomel, smiling mockingly.

The lion stood at the edge of the plateau, fiery eyes seething with rage, frustrated by Windgate's narrow escape, but reluctant to pursue along the ledge. Even with its anchoring talons, the narrow course would be a dangerous and tedious task, testing balance and strength together with no surviving a mistake.

Windgate stared at the great dark form and sneered.

"Too slow, beast!" he taunted. "Even Baalkor gave me a better run!"

Windgate bounded forward even as the lion roared, tensing to leap. And he was desperately scampering out of range as the colossal form collided against the cliff, its deafening roar thundering along the wall. Windgate risked a quick glance backwards to see that the lion was moving slowly after him on the narrow ledge, talons grasping securely at the black ice. And the hare bounded forward at the sight, defiantly determined to lure the beast to the hidden cave.

At the curve that hid the cleft, Windgate paused, turning, and saw that the lion was already upon him, hideous jaws gaping. The beast seemed to consider the big hare's curious maneuver as an act of surrender, and it smiled. But Windgate continued to retreat, drawing the beast carefully toward the cave.

The ledge was all but lost in the defeated light, and Windgate backed cautiously around the curve, allowing the lion to move even closer to him. And in moments it stood barely short of the cavern entrance, its fierce pride imperiously cloaking the dark visage.

"You are a fool!" it snarled, breathing blasts of black frost into the night. "Why does your kind still try to resist the Dark Lord? Don't you realize that we are superior? You and your kind are lost in dreams and visions, in fantasies that give you no power. You are weak. Your God is weak. That is why we shall destroy you from the Earth."

Only a small step remained before Incomel stood in front of the cave, but Windgate knew that nothing could be done until the beast made that final move. The hare stepped silently back, forcing the lion to move closer in order to strike its killing blow. And with the step Incomel also began to advance, then halted in midstride.

Incomel's feral eyes narrowed, suspicious, and Windgate realized that the lion, even though it could not yet see the cave, had somehow sensed a hidden threat. Motionless, unable to comprehend its sudden, disturbing fear, Incomel poised on the ledge. And Windgate knew he would have to move quickly or all would be lost.

Flesh shaking from the tension of the conflict, the hare searched for words that would cause the lion to complete its attack. Only moments remained, for even as they stood, Windgate could see Incomel considering a quick retreat.

"I saw you in the Abyss!" Windgate said scornfully. "I know you're afraid of the old wolf!"

A tension suddenly stiffened Incomel's powerful form.

"Ha!" Windgate spat. "You are the true weakling, Incomel! Your flesh is strong, but you're afraid of a wolf! Ha! A wolf! Proud Incomel is afraid of a wolf!"

Within the lion's eyes a volcanic wrath emerged, and Windgate could see its caution swept aside by the demonic powers dominating its flesh.

"Kill me if you can!" Windgate screamed, striking wildly at the lion, startling the beast with his impetuous attack. Then the big hare desperately leapt back. But Incomel was lightning and pounced upon him, landing fully in front of the cave.

Even as the lion leapt, Gianavel exploded, roaring, from the cleft. And though the wolf moved with blinding speed, the lion was faster, whirling to meet the attack, lashing out with a powerful blow that struck Gianavel's shoulder. The old wolf staggered, but his momentum carried his headlong rush, and he collided with the lion on the edge of the precipice in an avalanche of ice and snow that blasted Windgate wildly along the ledge.

Fangs struck fangs as the two massive shapes clinched and closed in a thunderous embrace, roaring and slashing with killing grace. Windgate smashed into the icy wall and rebounded toward the chasm, clawing desperately for a grip. Screaming, even as he slid over the edge, Windgate finally caught hold, hanging tenaciously onto the ledge. He looked up frantically to see Gianavel fighting with his back to the wall, and Incomel slashing fiercely for balance on the narrow ice.

Struggling with volcanic strength, Incomel's giant shoulders strained to throw Gianavel from the tactical advantage. And Windgate watched, spellbound, as Gianavel locked against the lion with savage resistance, countering its wrath with an equal brand of titanic strength. Slowly, frozen in that dark majesty of might, they rocked forward and back on the edge of the precipice; demonic power incarnate straining violently against a holy force forged long ago from spirit and flesh.

Incomel's rear talons slashed deep grooves in the ice, digging desperately for leverage. But Windgate thought he perceived, even in the slow rocking of the embrace, a slight slipping of the monster's grip. And the lion's eyes widened, as if it sensed, finally, a terrible deliverance to some inescapable judgment, long dreaded and long delayed.

Roaring, Gianavel's fangs tore free from Incomel's black coat, and the old wolf's eyes blazed with his words.

"Die as you've lived!" Gianavel snarled.

With a powerful effort, the old wolf twisted violently, and Incomel's talons snapped sharply off the edge, the dark form thrown sidelong across the ledge. A long foreleg lashed out, striking the ice with shattering force, but the lion's great weight had already descended beneath the rim. Face flaming in fear, the beast had time for one terrifying, high-pitched scream, as talons tore futile furrows in the ice, before it was gone.

♦   ♦   ♦

Silently, Windgate stood beside Gianavel, staring down into the chasm that had claimed the beast. But the darkness and the misting clouds concealed the true depth of the ravine.

The hare had listened carefully for the sound of Incomel's death at the base of the cliff, but no noise, however distant, had returned to the cavern entrance where they still stood.

Impulsively, Windgate kicked a chunk of ice from the ledge and scowled over the edge.

"I hope it was painful," he said.

Gianavel looked down at him, the gray eyes glazed with pain. Suddenly concerned, Windgate saw that the old wolf's shoulder was torn from a deep slash, with other cuts bleeding in the ragged mane. Windgate studied Gianavel's stern face and saw iron control wrestling to subdue the agony of those ravaging wounds, and the hare wondered how much longer the old wolf's strength could endure.

"What will we do now?" he asked.

"We can't wait any longer for the pack," Gianavel replied, and sighed. "We'll have to go in and find Aramus and his friend. And then we can try to escape into the forest. Perhaps if we can get into the woods, we'll meet the pack halfway."

The old wolf raised his head, gazing into the darkness, as if searching, before he spoke again.

"But it's night, and Baalkor is returning, if he hasn't already. So we have to go, and trust that the Lightmaker will make our way clear."

Windgate nodded.

"We will see what God will do," he said quietly.

t w e l v e

Guardians of the Abyss tracked the hare's scent through the stone corridor, growling, cursing the creature that had secretly entered their demonic domain.

Angry, suspicious, they hunted until they neared an all-but-forgotten section of the underground fortress: a long, jagged tunnel that led deep across the mountain to a dead and darkened end. Strangely, though, the air flowed more freely as they moved slowly forward, and the scent of snow was fresh in the dusky air.

Murderous eyes gleaming, the dark wolves explored the chamber, intent in their singular purpose to kill the intruder. But they neither saw nor sensed a presence beside them in the cave. Wolf scents were strong and fresh everywhere in the cavern, even here, and revealed nothing unusual. Yet when they discovered the un-guarded and unknown entrance, framed by night, the wolves noticed the tracks in the heavy snow; tracks of a wolf and a hare.

Staring at the lightning-torn sky, they did not see the massive shape behind them. While they gazed out into the darkness, it moved silently from the gloom at the far end of the tunnel, shadowed by a hare that moved with equal stealth. And in a moment the ghostly shapes were gone, disappearing into the corridor beyond.

♦ ♦ ♦

Aramus sensed the spirit long before he heard the quiet footfalls, his heart lifting with his silver eyes toward the darkened doorway. And in a moment the great gray wolf was there, inspiring and august, a faint smile gracing the aged face.

Aramus was beside his father before he even realized he had moved, and the old wolf nuzzled his neck affectionately, filling him with warmth and strength. But as they stood close, Aramus caught the scent of blood, and saw the massive wounds that marked his father's gray mane. Alarmed eyes looked intently at Gianavel, but the old wolf only shook his head, despising both the wounds and their power over him. And then Aramus caught the scent of Incomel.

"Incomel—" he began.

"Is dead," Gianavel said. "He died as he lived, in violence and pain. And now the Lightmaker will judge him for what he has done."

Aramus closed his eyes, breathing easier knowing that the beast was dead. And then he remembered Corbis.

"This is a trap," he whispered fiercely. "I told Windgate to warn you. They brought me here to lure you from the mountain so they can kill you."

"I know," said Gianavel. "But I'm not going to die until the Lightmaker allows me to die. Windgate is searching the Abyss for your friend, the bear. I will wait here, with you, until he finds him. Then we'll all try and escape together."

"But what if the guards return and discover us?"

"We'll deal with that when the time comes," said the old wolf. "But we won't lay down our lives to these fools."

Aramus stared at his father, estimating their chances.

"Are the Elders with you?" he asked.

"No," Gianavel replied. "We are alone. But the Lightmaker will deliver us."

Aramus glanced at the chamber door, breathing deeply. He felt charged for combat, even though they were heavily outnumbered. And when darkening thoughts arose in his mind, they were instantly cast down by the spirit that had re-created his heart and mind, strengthening him for the task.

Gianavel seemed to sense the change in his son, and Aramus watched the gray eyes focus upon him. "Your suffering has made you strong," said the old wolf. "I'm proud of you. You haven't turned away from what you believe. You stood the test of faith. You endured your suffering. Even in your pain, you did what you knew was right."

Gianavel hesitated, his eyes softening. And Aramus saw the true depth of love reflected in that aged face.

"We don't have much time, so words will be few," said his father. "But I may not survive this fight. And I've waited all your life to tell you what is on my heart."

With silver eyes gleaming, Aramus looked at the old gray wolf.

"From the day you were born, from the day your mother and I first looked upon you, we knew that you were here for a purpose. And I have feared for you, because I knew that the Lightmaker would make you strong so you could fulfill that purpose. And strength must be bought at a price.

"On the night that you saved Saul, I knew the Lightmaker was beginning a work within you. Even then, I knew that the old hare's death was not without reason. And I knew that there would be more to come, more suffering, more pain, until your heart and mind would be renewed. And I knew that it would be difficult for you. But I've prayed for you, hoping that when the dark night had finally passed, you would stand strong in the light. And I know that my prayers have been answered. You don't need me anymore. Your true life has begun. And the Lightmaker has many things he will want you to do, and you will do them by the strength within you."

Gianavel's gray head bent with his words, and the keen eyes clouded.

"We may have to fight to escape, but if I fall, don't come back for me. You must survive. You must escape.

I am old, and I've lived my life. But you're young, and your life is still before you. So you must live. But no matter what happens, always remember how much your father loved you."

Silver eyes gazed upon the old wolf, and Gianavel moved closer, devoted and loving. And for a long moment they stood, affectionate and embracing, and Aramus realized that these were the moments he had always cherished the most, the quiet moments when his father was soft and spoke through his heart. Aramus closed his eyes, feeling the warmth, the love, of the old wolf. And he knew the moment would live forever within him, even as Saul lived within him.

Frantic sounds in the corridor made them turn.

Gianavel had moved even before Aramus reacted. And when Aramus turned he saw Windgate standing, breathless, barely inside the room. The big hare was exhausted, struggling to speak.

"Wolves!" he panted, gasping. "Everywhere! . . . I never thought . . . I'd make it!"

Gianavel leapt lightly to the door, peered out, and turned to the big hare.

"Where's the bear?" he growled, ignoring Windgate's wild gesturing.

Windgate returned a shocked stare.

"Oh, thank you . . . yes, I'm fine . . . thank you . . . for asking."

Aramus gazed in astonishment as they scowled, like old friends, at one another. And he wondered briefly what strange ordeal had forged this bond.

Then Gianavel smiled down at the hare. "Good. I'm glad you're fine. Now where is the bear?"

Windgate pointed, exhausted, down the hall.

"But the wolves . . . know something. It's not like it was . . . last night. This place . . . is crawling with wolves. A bunch of them . . . are guarding the bear. And a bunch more . . . are coming this way. I think . . . Baalkor is with them."

"Let's move," said Gianavel, casting them both a stern glance before he looked again at Windgate.

"Take us to the bear."

t h i r t e e n

Silently Windgate led them down one corridor, and another, and at the sound of a patrol they leapt together into yet another shadowed tunnel that led only into another gloomy chamber. Aramus, mane bristling with tension, looked over his shoulder, wondering why the dark wolves had not already discovered Windgate by scent.

"Why aren't they hunting you by scent?" he whispered harshly.

"They are hunting me!" Windgate replied, eyes gleaming fiercely. "But I've been all over this place. Ha! My scent is in every one of these halls! Let's see 'em hunt that!"

Then the big hare was moving again, Gianavel and Aramus close behind. Windgate moved quickly but quietly, always finding a way through the treacherous, echoing halls that were slowly awakening with roars and monstrous shapes.

Guardians of the Abyss, clearly alerted to some invading force, were stalking, enraged, through the mazelike halls adjacent to the throne of Corbis. And Aramus sometimes caught sight of horrific shadows swaying eerily upon distant walls, wavering in the gloom for a long, threatening instant, before disappearing again into the cavernous shadows.

Aramus was vaguely amazed as he experienced in action the deeper strength that had come upon him. For even as he moved he felt a power working within, a power that went strangely beyond flesh. It seemed almost as if the entire essence of his heart, mind, and spirit had been transformed, enabling him to understand and overcome the weaknesses of his flesh. He knew a certain fear, but it was a dim, thin fear, overwhelmed by the force upon him, an empowering force that cleared his thoughts and cloaked him with a boldness, within and without.

Suddenly, without warning or sound, Windgate halted before a corner, Aramus and Gianavel a mirror of the hare's stance. Creeping forward with silent steps, Windgate cast a careful look around the curving black wall, then slid back cautiously. Eyes wide with excitement, he pointed, indicating the direction of Kaleel's holding place. And Gianavel moved forward to glance narrowly down the hall, then also eased back.

"A dozen guards," Gianavel said quietly. "We must strike quickly."

Aramus nodded, his blood thrilling for the fight.

"Kaleel will join us," he whispered.

"Good," replied Gianavel. "We'll need his strength."

Vengeful howls were booming along the length and breadth of the Abyss, and Gianavel suddenly raised his head, following the sounds before looking at Aramus again.

"They know where we are," he snarled. "They're coming for us. We don't have any more time."

Aramus nodded and looked at Windgate. "Get ready to run."

"Don't worry," whispered the hare.

Father and son locked eyes for a breath, and even in the tension of that moment, with dark forces closing upon them, Gianavel's affection blazed through his heated gray gaze.

"There's no one I would rather have beside me," the old wolf said softly.

Aramus's heart was racing, fiercely preparing his body for combat. But still, a flood of emotion welled within him at his father's words. He smiled at the old wolf, nodding, and moved beside his father as they rounded the corner.

Roaring, they rushed the guards who turned, snarling, against them. Gianavel collided against a great black form, driving the creature back before his terrifying aspect. And Aramus crashed full into the fray, shouting to Kaleel.

For a flashing instant the bear reeled, shocked, on hind legs, as if unable to comprehend the moment.

Then with a vengeful roar he burst forth from the chamber and into the corridor with sweeping blows.

Feeling alone and abandoned, the bear's fighting instinct had abated in the presence of the surrounding wolves. But now, with friends beside him and doom forestalled, his volcanic strength was again ignited to erupt into the hallway in a terrifying display of savage power.

In moments, three of the dark shapes lay writhing on the floor. And the rest, terrified that they had been met with equal force, turned and fled, their angry cries following them down the long corridor.

Even as the dark wolves retreated, Aramus spun toward Kaleel. "We've got to hurry!" he shouted above the resounding, retreating howls.

"Where is Incomel?" roared Kaleel, froth scattering with the terrible words. "Where is Incomel? He shall pay for my father's blood!"

"He's dead!" shouted Aramus, trying to still Kaleel's fighting madness.

"Incomel!" Kaleel roared. "Where is Incomel?"

Aramus leapt directly in front of the bear and shouted into his face.

"Kaleel! He's dead! He's dead!"

Slowly, the dark eyes blinked at Aramus, even as the bear swayed from side to side. And Aramus could see that his friend was shocked and angry at the news, frustrated that his suicidal energy to face Incomel in combat once again could not be released.

"We have to get out here!" Aramus continued. "Corbis is still alive, and he'll kill us all! We have to escape while we can! To fight is to die. We can't defeat them."

Kaleel's glaring gaze shifted at shadows, searching for something upon which he could unleash his wrath. Then, with a trembling effort, Aramus saw him attempting to still the rage within. Shaking, the bear turned toward Gianavel, who was staring intently down the corridor.

"This is my father," Aramus whispered. "Now, let's get out of here. There are too many of them to fight."

His anger slightly abated, Kaleel accepted the words without question, seeming to know already that the old gray wolf bore him no harm. He nodded his head.

"This way!" shouted Windgate, poised in an empty hallway. "This will take us out!"

Kaleel was instantly beside Aramus, and seemed neither to notice nor to care about the strange alliance with the hare.

Windgate, leading the escape, fairly flew down the subterranean halls, moving with expert skill over jagged rock and darkened pit as quickly as wolf ever could in the close confines of the corridor.

Racing against the doom descending upon them, the four fled through a chamber that led off into a dozen connecting corridors. Windgate instantly selected a sloping tunnel that ran uphill, drawing wind from the mountain. But howls were fast closing upon them, wolves cutting off every avenue of escape. And as they sped into another shadowy chamber, Windgate slid to a halt, livid, as the tunnel before them suddenly echoed with fiendish cries.

"They've closed it off!" he yelled, turning toward them. "We can't get out!"

Aramus whirled, snarling, as wolves exploded into the chamber they had just exited, thundering into the distant room in a roaring storm of murderous rage.

"Follow me!" Gianavel shouted above the din, charging down another hall.

Without hesitation they closed behind the old wolf. Aramus pulled alongside his father, Kaleel behind, with Windgate bounding quickly at the back. And then Aramus heard a deafening chorus coming toward them from the opposite end of the tunnel, howls that seemed to sense their approach, despising their strength.

"They're coming straight for us!" Aramus yelled.

Gianavel's gray eyes blazed, and his words were swallowed by the wind that swept across them. "They're trying to block all the tunnels that lead to the outside! We have to break through them!"

Aramus stretched out his stride, and together father and son flew forward, shoulder to shoulder, down the hall. While from the other end of the corridor a demonic horde emerged hauntingly from the gloom, red eyes blazing and separated fangs streaming froth, hurtling toward them with hungry cries.

Gianavel roared defiantly and threw himself forward with a speed that left Aramus back a stride. But even as the old wolf surged ahead, Kaleel swept up to take his

place, charging alongside Aramus's silver mane. And
with Gianavel leading the thunderous wedge, they
collided against the onrushing pack.

Instantly the corridor exploded in a maelstrom of
roars and blows that raged wildly from narrow wall to
narrow wall. Aramus struck again and again, submerged
in dark forms that slashed and struck against him in
return. But Aramus had been lifted beyond pain, beyond
fear, and he attacked anything that rose against him,
drawing blood and tearing away flesh, lost in the fury of
wounds delivered and wounds received.

And Gianavel, unleashing the full fury of his fighting
rage, struck but once at a dark wolf before the gray one
whirled, hurling the dying shape to the dust. No longer
restrained by the spirit within, but compelled to unleash
his wrath upon those who had provoked that wrath, the
old wolf was the image of death, destroying with cold
skill while the gray eyes blazed forth a terrifying aspect
of purpose. And none who rose against him lived to
retreat.

But even as Aramus was cascaded with blows and
mortally locked with a monstrous black shape, he
glimpsed Kaleel also wreaking a savage score. The bear
seemed gigantic in the gloom, roaring and striking and
tearing with wide, killing swipes of the heavy paws that
shattered flesh and bone alike. And almost before
Aramus realized what had happened, they had burst
through, scattering demonic shapes wildly before their
combined wrath.

Burning with the exhausting effort of their escape, they staggered past the shattered line, down the narrow corridor, and toward the chamber that loomed beyond.

"Wait!" screamed Aramus, and Gianavel cast a frantic look back. "Where's Windgate?"

"I'm here!" the hare shouted excitedly, far ahead of where they stood. Aramus whirled, too fatigued and enraged from combat to imagine how the hare had slid through the wildly chaotic conflict. He leaped up to Windgate and, without conscious effort or thought, leaned down to touch the small form with his nose.

"Not again," Aramus whispered, more to himself than to his newfound friend. "Not again. . . ."

Silver eyes gazed into brown, and Windgate smiled. And together they turned, emerging from the corridor into a cavern.

Aramus knew instantly where he was, and his eyes locked on the granite throne of Corbis that dominated the Abyss. It was empty. And across the huge chamber Aramus saw the shadowed entrance of the tunnel that led to the icy slope and the path down the mountain. He turned to his father.

"That's the tunnel that leads outside!"

Gianavel cast an electrified glance at the entrance before turning blazing eyes toward the corridor they had fled. Howls left behind when they burst through the dark wolves had turned and were rapidly converging upon the main hall.

"We'll fight them on the ice!" the old wolf snarled, his voice charged with rage. "Everybody get outside!"

As one they turned, hearing the gathering cries closing quickly upon the hall, but seeing the way clear to escape. And then it was there.

A prehistoric roar thundered across them as the Beast emerged, demonic jaws distended, from the shadows beside the tunnel, the tunnel that had promised escape and freedom, yet which now promised only a cruel and painful death.

Monolithic, cloaked in darkness, Corbis towered in the Abyss, baleful eyes glaring upon them with a wrath lost to the Earth since the beginning of time. And for a moment, as they stood frozen in the spectral scene, Aramus saw the bear as more than flesh. It was the Dark Lord Incarnate, that Dragon of Ancient Lore, the Destroyer of Worlds.

f o u r t e e n

Corbis growled, trembling rock deep into
the mountain and sending a heated wave
of concentrated hate to the cavernous walls, charging
the atmosphere until the air vibrated with murderous
intent.

Gianavel alone was undaunted and returned a savage
snarl, fully into the face of the Beast. And Aramus,
awakened from his shock by his father's stance, was
instantly beside the old wolf, fangs clicking fiendishly in
defiance.

Corbis glared upon them, cold and overpowering, the
proud image of primeval might. Then the hateful gaze
blazed with scornful mirth as dark wolves suddenly swept
in from the myriad corridors, thronging the Abyss.

Instantly Gianavel and Aramus were back to back,
with Kaleel turning also to face outward against their

encircling foes. And Windgate fell to the middle of the trio, helpless against such powerful beasts.

A cacophony of roars and screams thundered across the Abyss as the opposing forces waged a ghostly war of attacks thrown and attacks withdrawn, with never fang meeting flesh.

Gianavel's bristling presence threw their attackers back a wide space. For even though the dark horde knew that, in force, they could drag the old wolf to the ground, they also knew that the first to touch that gray shape would surely die.

Aramus imitated his father, learning breath by breath how to stand in such a fight. And Kaleel repeatedly struck at elusive shapes that leapt in and out, reluctant to receive the impact of those crushing paws. For a spellbinding moment the battle raged until a thunderous command shattered the chaos.

"Hold!" roared Corbis.

Instantly the dark wolves responded to the brutal voice, obediently falling back, tension slowly fading from the snarling faces. And after a moment the surrounded servants of the Lightmaker stood within a narrow gap of safety, clear to turn their attention from the wolves to the Beast that commanded them.

"At last we meet...the great Gianavel!" Corbis growled, breathless. "I am...amazed...that you have survived so long. Speak with me, old wolf, before I destroy you! Make me afraid! Reveal to me the strength that makes proud Incomel tremble!"

Gianavel turned his dauntless head toward Corbis. Yet the old wolf did not speak, his entire aspect smoldering with an intensity of wrath that rendered him speechless while simultaneously communicating an unconquerable resistance. And then slowly, with a rising control, Gianavel's electrifying rage seemed to lessen, calmed by the spirit that never lost dominion over that disciplined flesh. And the gray eyes gazed upon the Beast, measuring something, some argument to come, seeming to know already the direction of words yet unspoken and perceiving the bitter outcome.

Gianavel's stance was as solid as his words.

"Incomel feared me because he knew that the spirit within me proclaimed his doom," he growled. "As it proclaims yours."

Visibly moved in his dark aspect, Corbis glared upon them. The Beast seemed to search Gianavel's words, and the malevolent gaze wavered, as if beholding something beyond the Abyss.

"Can it be?" whispered Corbis, shaken. "Incomel... destroyed?"

Gianavel nodded, the gray face stern.

"Incomel is dead," he said coldly. "And he was not cast down by flesh. It was the one least in strength who lured the lion to his doom."

Corbis focused scornfully upon Windgate.

"O... most horrible," the Beast whispered. "The weak have destroyed... the strong."

Gianavel's quiet voice rang unnaturally clear into every corner of the cavern.

"As it was meant to be, Corbis. And it was not mortal strength that defeated the lion. It was the power of the Lightmaker that delivered his doom. For your evil has caught up to you, Beast. Despite our weakness and your great strength, I proclaim to you that, from this night forward, the Dark Council will terrify no more. Even tonight, in this very hour, you yourself will be destroyed, struck down by the wrath of God."

Corbis's dark gaze clouded, as with a gathering thunderstorm. And a silent rage danced like crimson flames in the hateful eyes. Imperceptibly, the colossus crouched, a visible strength building volcanically in its enormous form.

Soundlessly, from the shadow of the giant bear, Baalkor stalked forth, hideous head lowered and murderous gaze burning red in the gloom. As ferocious, as horrible as before, Baalkor fixed a hungry stare upon Aramus and separated its savage fangs, smiling.

Even as he caught sight of the dark wolf, Aramus snarled, mane bristling. And in a defiant struggle they tested strength of soul and spirit, growls vibrating the granite floor that stretched between them.

Aramus realized, even as he reacted, that he was no longer afraid of the dark wolf. And he struggled not to leap forward into battle, knowing that he should not move until his father moved. For wisdom must lead, not strength. And with the thought he began to still his growl, slowing the shuddering vibrations until he stood again in silence, his eyes locked against Baalkor's.

Corbis ignored the deadly tension, continuing to glare balefully upon Gianavel.

"Strength is on our side, old wolf," he growled. "Your God has forsaken you!"

Gianavel frowned at the Beast.

"We will see who is forsaken," he said.

"Your God has forsaken you!" roared Corbis, stepping forward. "What do you see, Gianavel? Tell me what you see! You are surrounded. There is no one to defend you against my strength. The Lightmaker is not here! He is not here because your heart is evil! Yes, Gianavel, you are evil! Behold, old wolf! Behold the darkness that rules your heart! Behold . . . the power of the Dark Lord!"

Corbis's incarnate power swept across the Abyss, and the darkness wavered, trembling with the force unleashed within. The shadows moved, condensing about Gianavel, shrouding him in darkness, focusing the full persuasive power of its hellish intensity upon the great gray wolf.

Aramus watched as Corbis swayed in the gloom, his dark soul becoming one with the otherworldly force that descended upon his father.

Gianavel stood motionless, the gray face unreadable, holding Corbis's demonic gaze. Then, still glaring at the Beast, the great wolf lowered his head, and it seemed as if a mortal cloak suddenly fell away, revealing an awesome and unearthly presence, beyond the world's power to defy or destroy. Instantly the darkness surrounding the old wolf faded, fleeing into the shadows of the Abyss.

Gianavel smiled.

"The Dark Lord has no power over me, Corbis."

Roaring, the Beast smashed a gigantic paw upon a granite slab, and the stone shattered at the impact, sending a shock wave to the cavernous walls.

"You are a fool, Gianavel!" roared Corbis. "You are a fool! Do you really think your pitiful strength can conquer the Dark Lord! You are weak! Your kind have always been weak! I will destroy you!"

"Know this, Corbis!" snarled Gianavel, mane bristling with the words. "The Lightmaker will destroy you tonight! And flesh shall not bring you down! Despite your great strength, the Lightmaker proclaims that the Dark Council will terrify no more!"

A madness possessed the Beast even as Gianavel's words were spoken, and the creature roared forth from the darkness, emerging fully in the ghastly light.

Scorning all strength but its own, Corbis towered in the Abyss. As if carved from black granite, its flesh was displayed; flesh hard with rocklike strength and armored within a thick mane of shaggy fur. And its limbs, heavy and massive with muscle, flexed, commanding the power to shatter stone and mountain alike. At the end of the massive paws, threatening stands of razorlike claws extended into the air, keen and cruel, unnaturally long and gleaming with an edge that knew no resistance in earthly substance.

Corbis's colossal head looked down upon them, and the great fangs parted, revealing arching rows of white death. Then a thunderous growl gathered intensity, trembling the mountain deep into the earth, until the hideous jaws savagely separated, blasting a deafening roar across them. The hot wave submerged Aramus within its hateful wrath, and his snarl was lost in the dark wind that swept past.

"Now you will know strength, Gianavel!"

A fiendish howl hurled from the rear of the cavern tore through the Abyss, a howl of pain and escape, followed by the chaotic cries of a savage conflict. Automatically Aramus spun toward the wounded cry before realizing that, despite the violent distraction, Gianavel had never taken his eyes off Corbis. Understanding instantly, Aramus whirled back toward his father and the Beast, and though he stood only a heartbeat away, he could never say which moved first, or fastest.

fifteen

Corbis struck a rending blow, but Gianavel was no longer there, leaping sideways to evade the great black claws that slashed a murderous arc through the darkened air.

Aramus snatched Windgate up with a blinding movement that evaded Baalkor's crushing rush and was gone, bounding long to land before a wall of snarling dark wolves that barred his way. With steel strength Aramus hit the floor and launched himself high again, carrying the helpless hare far over the heads of the encircling wolves to land lightly upon the throne of Corbis. In a flash he dropped Windgate over the far side to land unharmed, far from the raging battle.

"Hide!" said Aramus, and Windgate was gone, vanishing amidst the rubble as only he could do.

Aramus whirled, and in a flashing moment saw that the Elders of the Gray Wolves had finally arrived,

charging into the Abyss through the hidden entrance
that Windgate and Gianavel had followed. Across the
length and breadth of the cavern the gray wolves
clinched and closed with demonic shapes, and the air
resounded with roars and screams and desperate cries.
But Aramus had no more time to behold the sight. He
turned toward Gianavel, knowing that his father would
be fighting savagely with Corbis, only to see Death upon
him in a hurtling rush.

Baalkor struck him full force, blasting Aramus from
the throne and into the roaring air beyond. Aramus
locked up with the dark wolf even as they sailed through
space, and before they crashed to the granite floor they
were revolving in a merciless exchange of slashing blows.

Aramus twisted violently before they struck the stone,
punishing Baalkor with the impact. And then they were
gone, slashing with blows that, had even one struck
true, would have ended the battle with its killing force.
But in the swirling, spinning, maelstrom of movement
each saw the other's blow and evaded, by the slightest,
flashing margin, that measure of accuracy that would
have severed his neck.

So involved was Aramus in the battle that he had no
time to think of his father. Baalkor was all over him,
snarling and striking with a fury flamed by rage from his
earlier defeat. And Aramus returned the same with a
fighting skill he had never known, not even in their
earlier conflict. For then, even in his rage, he had been
afraid of the dark wolf, and the fear had tied up his
heart and mind. Nor had he been experienced in the art

of war. Now, with a purity of heart and a freedom of mind, Aramus forced the battle to the beast, unleashing his purer intensity with a directness of movement that struck unimpeded by fear or the rage that blinds. He struck deep, and he struck true, and his shining silver eyes never left the target of his wrath.

Yet despite his fierce intensity Aramus heard a familiar howl tear through the dusky air. Struck by the sound, he violently threw Baalkor back to gain a space and glared across the chamber.

Upon the dark throne Corbis reared above the fallen Gianavel, injured at last. The bear roared triumphantly, and Aramus turned toward the throne. Then Baalkor was on him again, the stunning impact taking Aramus in a slashing frenzy across the cavern floor, rolling in a deadly embrace with the beast until they disappeared into the tunnel beyond.

◆ ◆ ◆

"Die, Gianavel!" roared Corbis, the black claws raised high above the wounded form. "Now you know why the Dark Lord rules the Earth!"

Windgate was before Corbis even as Gianavel saw the big hare leap upon the dark throne. Corbis, astonished, glared down at the hare, as if unable to comprehend the defiant act.

"Doom is upon you, Corbis!" shouted Windgate, raising onto hind legs to face the Beast. "Saul's death has destroyed you!"

Corbis roared, claws descending, but the hare leaped straight between the treelike legs to land behind the Beast. Then an avalanche of gray wolves, led by the ancient Razul, descended upon the dark throne in a roaring storm.

In a spinning silver wheel they revolved around the Beast, striking and tearing with disciplined skill, drawing the monster's attention from their fallen king until Gianavel finally staggered up from the bloody throne to launch himself again into the attack.

Corbis was cascaded with gray, fearsome wolves of hardened strength that struck true and leaped away—old wolves skilled in war and dauntless in courage. Yet twice the descending black claws cut though the smoking air and caught a massive gray shape, hurling the Elder through the air to land limply in the dust. And with each death the others increased the raging attack, slashing all that they could reach of the towering shape. They leaped boldly upon the Beast, striking at neck and head and face to drag the monster to the ground. And even more were wounded in the effort, hurled through the air and broken by the fearsome jaws. Until, finally tearing loose from a swarm of dark wolves on the cavern floor, Kaleel leaped upon the throne and ascended the steps with a directness of purpose that tore Corbis's attention from his attackers.

Gianavel saw Kaleel's intent and knew that Corbis would crush the smaller bear with its first shattering blow. And with the thought the old wolf leaped high to strike Corbis, slashing a wound above a glaring eye.

Corbis roared and swung a powerful paw through the air, smashing Gianavel against the wall. And then Kaleel struck, the lean claws cutting an arc through the pale light to slice across Corbis's neck. And the blow continued, the claws tearing a deep path through fur and flesh and whatever was beneath to enter the air in a trail of black haze.

Roaring demonically, Corbis wheeled and returned the blow. Its massive paw lashed out and caught Kaleel in the chest, blasting the smaller bear from the throne with the thunderous impact, and Kaleel screamed as he crashed across the cavern floor.

Then Corbis turned against the gray wolves with an insanity of wrath that ignored all pain and drove him relentlessly after Gianavel. As one force the Elders fought back, knowing Corbis's singular desire to slay their king, while Corbis pressed forward in his hellish power, striking gray forms from the throne and the air with uncanny skill.

◆ ◆ ◆

Aramus cast a desperate glance past Baalkor to see the fantastic battle on the throne. Elders swirled about Corbis, but were falling quickly before the killing blows that split the air with rending cries of violent death. And Aramus knew that, if not finished soon, Corbis would live to finish Gianavel, and perhaps all of them.

Baalkor struck him again and Aramus went back beneath the weight. Together they rolled, each striking desperately for the blow that would finish the fight and end at last this hated conflict. Aramus retreated before Baalkor's slashing storm, breath heaving in gasps as he struggled to survive. Deep fatigue made his legs slow to respond, and his eyes were blurred with the exhausting effort of the fight.

"You were a fool to stand against me!" growled Baalkor between blows. "I'll kill you like I killed Saul!"

Aramus's silver eyes blazed.

"Saul defeated you!" he snarled. "And I defeated you!"

Baalkor roared and struck him again, slashing deep. Aramus returned the blow but fell back again, retreating even further into the tunnel, away from Gianavel who was struggling to regain his feet on the throne.

"Corbis is killing your father!" roared Baalkor, laughing. "Help him! All you have to do is . . . get . . . past . . . me!"

Another injured howl from Gianavel tore through the tomb.

"Father!" screamed Aramus.

Baalkor struck again, forcing Aramus back before its superior strength. Livid with rage, Aramus slashed the dark wolf high in its scarred face, and Baalkor instinctively stepped back. Hope flaming at the reaction, Aramus pressed his attack, and Baalkor began to slowly retreat.

Aramus increased his force, striking blow upon blow, and Baalkor was driven before the onslaught. Somewhere in the enveloping pain Aramus lost all touch with the earth, knowing only heat and blood and the burning of his exhausted flesh. There was only the blow, the lunge, the slash, even as a consuming heaviness began to overcome his defiant will. But in his fierce love Aramus ignored the pain and forced his flesh to do what must be done, driving the dark prince before him until finally they stood in the entrance of the Abyss.

Aramus faltered, hesitating at last, his lungs burning as deeply as wounds had ever burned his flesh. And Baalkor swayed in the tunnel gloom, still blocking his way while slashed to pieces by his wrath. Aramus's face twisted in disbelief, and he knew that if he did not strike a finishing blow, the dark wolf's endless strength would outlast him.

"You cannot . . . destroy me," snarled Baalkor, breathing heavily. "I'll live . . . to kill you, and your father. Your love . . . makes you weak."

Silver eyes narrowed at the words and Aramus snarled, lowering his head, focusing on the dark wolf. This was the end, he knew, for a fight so terrible could not endure.

Aramus leaped, bridging the gap without warning. He feinted high, then lunged beneath Baalkor's defense and tore open its chest. Aramus felt ribs and flesh surrender to the blow, and the dark wolf staggered back, howling a mortal cry. Distracted by the crippling pain, Baalkor never saw the fangs that closed upon his foreleg. A wrenching twist of powerful jaws snapped the leg and Aramus instantly released, evading the returning slash that missed his face by a narrow edge.

Roaring in pain, Baalkor reared back, snarling, and the maddened eyes blazed at Aramus, who edged closer.

Baalkor cast a wild look over his shoulder.

"I will return," it rasped, choked by its pain. "And I will destroy you."

Aramus gazed into the demonic eyes, saw the unending hate, and suddenly beheld a scene far from the Abyss. Even as Aramus stood before the Beast, he gazed upon a moonlit glade where an old hare lay dying in the snow, faithful and loving to the end . . . and he saw Windgate, standing brokenly over the body of his fallen friend . . . Kaleel mourning the loss of his father . . . Gianavel wounded beneath Corbis. And not even Aramus knew what deep purpose decided his reply, but his words fell like ice from white fangs.

"No," he said. "This is the end."

Aramus moved forward, slowly at first, and Baalkor saw the lethal light of those silver eyes. The dark wolf snarled hideously, and Aramus moved again, faster, his movements blending suddenly into a blinding, silver blur that swept in with supernatural speed.

Baalkor saw the silver shape sweep in and sweep out again, and felt with the movement a numbness descend instantly upon him. He staggered, the evil face a mask of shock and disbelief, and felt his strength spilling onto the cavern floor.

A moment more he stood, staring at the silver wolf, who watched, breathing hard, only a step away. Then suddenly, as if summoned by a force beyond his will, the dark wolf stumbled, collapsing.

Baalkor looked up and saw Aramus standing over
him, the silver eyes somehow saddened, shocked at the
horror of the task. Then he felt the sentence of death,
and in the final, terrifying moment beheld an unearthly
judgment crowning that silver brow, before darkness
claimed him.

Even as the dark head fell, Aramus turned away,
leaping into the cavern to meet Kaleel rising from the
floor. The bear staggered up slowly, dazed and disoriented from a terrible wound. No words were passed
as the friends met, and none were necessary as they
turned and quickly ascended the granite to enter the
battle on the throne.

Unable to wait for Kaleel, Aramus ran forward to
see Gianavel pinned against a flat wall, inescapably
trapped by Corbis's wide reach. Elders swirled about the
Beast, striking and roaring, but Corbis was returning
their wrath and more while sweeping wide, killing blows
that Gianavel evaded by the narrowest edge.

Roaring, Aramus bounded up the throne and
launched himself high with a powerful leap. Corbis
turned, struck by the challenge, as Aramus completed a
silver arc through the shadowy air and descended, fangs
announcing his intent, into the face of the Beast.

Aramus saw the gaping wound in Corbis's massive neck as he descended and knew he would only have time for a single blow. And even as he landed his fangs lashed out, tearing a deeper wound through the wound already there. Corbis roared, snatching Aramus between massive paws, and hurled him with stunning force into the wall beside Gianavel.

Corbis descended upon them, ignoring the Elders who threw themselves into the fight with suicidal abandon, slashing with exhausted strength. And then Kaleel leaped forward, roaring, to strike yet another blow at the injured neck.

Corbis spun at the slashing blow and returned the attack, lashing out with unbelievable force. The huge paw struck Kaleel's shoulder, shattering flesh and bone together, and the young bear cried out, staggering back wildly from the crushing impact. Turned from Gianavel

by the threat of yet another and perhaps fatal blow from
the young bear, Corbis leaped upon Kaleel to finish the
kill.

Struck with horror, Aramus and Gianavel roared and
leaped together upon Corbis. Aramus slashed at the
monster's shoulder, tearing away the dark fur, and
Gianavel, defying Corbis's deadly jaws, sank fangs deep
into the rending wound that had been torn by Kaleel,
breaking the Beast from the ravaging attack.

Corbis roared, whirled toward Gianavel and leaped
forward, but the old wolf was gone, striking a rear leg
and leaping back again, using his superior speed and
evasiveness to every advantage. Corbis advanced after
him, while Kaleel staggered slowly to his feet, bleeding
and stunned.

Upon the dark throne they circled the Beast, and in a
flashing, nightmarish conflict waged a devastating battle
of attacks thrown and countered, of blows delivered and
blows received and fangs returning the same. Then
Corbis launched a sweeping rush toward Gianavel.
Almost, the old wolf evaded the closing force, but a
wide paw caught him in the side. Gianavel roared
savagely as the crushing blow hurled him across the
throne, where he collapsed.

Corbis rushed forward to throw another killing swipe
of the black claws. But even as the Beast moved,
Aramus leaped in with suicidal boldness. His long fangs
sank deep into the bear's neck and Aramus leaped back
again, tearing away the dark flesh. Roaring in agony,
Corbis reared, towering above them all, and turned

toward Aramus, who backed out upon the throne, snarling and roaring in his own rage.

Fangs smoking with blood, the Beast bent over the silver wolf and roared, scorning the power of its wound. And Aramus looked fully into Corbis's unearthly eyes, beholding the world contained within the blackened depths, a world darkly solid and pure with evil purpose, covered by dancing slivers of demonic life.

"I will destroy you!" Corbis rasped.

Aramus stared into the eyes, shook his head.

"No," he gasped, "you'll only destroy my flesh."

Corbis roared and raised the black claws high, and then Gianavel struck.

The great gray wolf collided against the Beast with devastating force, striking high and true to draw deep blood, and Corbis's killing blow was lost within the impact. Then Kaleel leaped forward, locking teeth deeply into Corbis's huge foreleg, using all his weight to drag the monster down.

Staggering, resisting the roaring attack with primordial strength, Corbis attempted to shake off Kaleel, and struck wildly at the elusive gray shape of Gianavel. And Aramus, with Razul beside him, leaped into the attack.

Blow after blow, they weakened the Beast. Corbis slashed at Kaleel, who howled in agony but grimly refused to release his grip. Frustrated and enraged to madness, Corbis struck again at the wolves. The Beast's black claws descended in a wide arc, and in a terrific instant collided against Razul's side, hurling the lean gray wolf from the throne.

Aramus and Gianavel watched Razul smash against the cavern floor, but even as he landed, the old wolf staggered blindly up, bleeding and coughing, and they knew he would survive. Yet when they turned again to Corbis, Gianavel launched himself into the attack with a fury and rage that made even Aramus shrink back.

With supernatural strength, eternal moment by eternal moment, blow upon blow, Gianavel slashed wildly at the Beast. The cavern floor streamed with blood and Corbis struck with monstrous strength, yet it did not lessen the fury of their combined attack. Lungs burning, legs deadened by the exhausting fury of the conflict, father and son drove themselves forward, refusing to surrender to the fatigue that devoured their strength.

And, finally, when Aramus had begun to fear that nothing would ever weaken Corbis's colossal might, he felt the slightest lessening in its stance. Heart and hope suddenly strengthened, Aramus threw himself into the final moment of the fight with wild abandon, pushing his strength that last step, forced his failing limbs to strike again and again, refusing to rest his burning lungs and legs, doing all that flesh could do. Then Corbis suddenly staggered, and with Kaleel hanging tenaciously from a foreleg, fell across the granite.

Aramus was lost in the blinding flurry of fangs and blows that followed through the next chaotic instant. As long as he lived, he would only remember black claws sweeping over him and the forms of Gianavel and Kaleel as they struck time after time. Aramus fought on, knowing nothing but his wounds and the burning and the blood that clouded his sight.

Yet he would never forget how Corbis, enraged by some final instinct of death and empowered by that dark strength that drained the stars of life, suddenly threw them off together, and against all natural force began to rise from the cavern floor. Shocked and exhausted from the destroying effort of the fight, Aramus fell back, roaring in anger and frustration as the colossal shape rose, its strength gathering even as it staggered up from the bloody stone. And gazing upon that dark majesty of might, Aramus feared that perhaps, indeed, the Beast could not be destroyed.

Then suddenly he was there: Gianavel, old and bloodied, alone before the Beast.

"It's over, Corbis," Gianavel gasped. "God proclaims . . . that you will terrify . . . no more."

Corbis laughed through a bloody froth.

"Your God . . . is weak, Gianavel! You . . . are weak!"

Dark blood masked Gianavel's fangs as he spoke.

"No, Beast," the old wolf shook his head. "The Lightmaker has destroyed you . . . at last."

Corbis began to rise, snarling, laughing.

"Not . . . by your God, Gianavel!" Corbis roared. "Not by your God!"

Gianavel struck again. Fully into the face of the Beast he leaped, tearing again at the ravaged wound. Yet in order to deliver the blow, the old wolf was forced to receive the same. Corbis closed a crushing embrace around Gianavel, and roaring in some abysmal agony of death, staggered up from the granite.

Aramus screamed as Corbis's great fangs separated and descended vengefully into the great wolf. And the two shapes swayed in the Abyss, crowned by roars and cries of the cavernous battle that lent an unearthly aspect to the scene, as if their spirits, more enduring and stronger than flesh, were continuing the conflict. Then suddenly, as if thunderously struck from above by some devastating power beyond them all, Corbis screamed, stumbling. Instantly Gianavel fell from the crushing embrace, rolling away as he hit the stone to leap clear.

Corbis swayed in the Abyss, grasping futilely at the blackness that cascaded down his colossal form. And he leaned against the darkness, reaching toward the vaulted ceiling as if beckoning to some otherworldly power that had finally forsaken him, at last. Then, with a slow, mountainous descent, the Beast crashed across his earthly throne.

seventeen

Grievously wounded, Gianavel watched, with Aramus beside him, as the dark wolves were beaten back and routed. Unleashing the full measure of their wrath, the vengeful Elders struck down demonic shapes even as they fled, driving them deeper into the corridors of the glacial mountain.

Windgate was standing beside him before Aramus heard the hare's quiet footsteps. Aramus looked down to see Windgate carefully studying Corbis, peering at the gaping fangs and glaring eyes, now fixed forever in a ghastly stare. The hare nodded softly to himself, as if measuring the rightness of the end. Then Windgate raised his face toward Aramus, smiling. And despite the pain of his own great wounds, Aramus felt himself smiling back in return.

Kaleel and Razul lay down beside them, moving slowly and painfully. Kaleel's shoulder was torn and broken, but he could move with a halting gait, and Aramus knew the bear's stout courage would overcome his wound. Razul bore a terrible injury, and moved even more slowly, but his old eyes smoldered fiercely in the faint light, undying and defiant, and Aramus knew that he, too, would survive the conflict.

Finally, when the remaining Elders had finished the fight, they moved also to the throne, surrounding the dead form of Corbis. Each gray shape was torn and slashed, yet Gianavel's wounds were the greatest, and he bore them the lightest, seeming to neither notice nor care about his wounded flesh, the fatigue of his gray eyes pierced from within by an enduring light, keen and commanding.

Solemnly, he gazed about the room.

"The price . . . was great," the old wolf said softly. "Those who have fallen . . . will be honored. And in the world to come, they will be glorified."

Gianavel looked into each weary face.

"Never forget this hour. It was the hour when you stood your ground, enduring the great test of suffering. Despite your pain, despite your weakness, you did what you knew was right. And I know that the battle was fierce. But you were brave, and you stood to the last. And now we must not grow weary. For an end to our suffering is in sight, and the Lightmaker's grace will sustain us."

Gianavel nodded to Aramus, delegating his authority.

"Let us leave this place of death," the old wolf said.

With Windgate beside him, Aramus led the pack up
the subterranean hall that led to the icy ridge. Aramus
remained intently alert for an ambush, but the caverns
and the halls and the Abyss were void of danger,
shrouded in utter defeat. Gianavel and Razul followed
slowly, surrounded and protected by fearsome Elders.

In force, they emerged into the early dawn, full into a
cold north wind that howled across the blackened ridge.
The mountain seemed angry at their victory, and slashed
them cruelly with sleet and ice, but they ignored its
wrath.

Leading the way, Aramus guided them skillfully
through the darkness, down the dangerous trail. As he
moved, he perceived that everything appeared different,
somehow. The trail was not so difficult, nor so cruel.
And he negotiated the descent with easy grace, careful
to keep the pace measured and slow.

In time they reached the base of the mountain,
moving from beneath the dark clouds, emerging into the
morning sun. Defensive to the last, they crossed the
landscape, prepared, always prepared, for some unseen
danger, some hidden threat. But there was nothing. The
power of darkness had been broken, unable to withstand
the ancient strength that had descended upon it. And
Aramus noticed that the land was strangely brighter,
warmer, than before.

At a ridgecrest Aramus and Windgate suddenly
turned, touched in their spirits, to look back at the
darkened mountain. All the others, unaware of the

sensation, continued past them, until the silver wolf and the hare stood alone, side by side, atop the barren hill.

In the distance they saw that a high, vengeful wind had come against the storming darkness of the mountain. And the wind, fiercer and stronger in the higher reaches of the sky, tore at the storm clouds until the darkness was slashed with light from the ascending sun.

Yet as he watched the darkness fall before the glowing dawn, Aramus's mind turned away from the mountain, and he thought solemnly of Saul. He looked down at Windgate, and the big hare gazed up, dark eyes softening, and Aramus knew that Windgate, too, was remembering their fallen friend, even as they heard the quiet words that whispered with the wind . . .

"Always strength comes. . . ."

With shining silver eyes Aramus watched as conquering white clouds rushed across the sky, driven by the relentless wind, sweeping over the mountain until the ice and the storm and the darkness together were overcome by the Light.

e p i l o g u e

Long years passed and Aramus was climbing a snow-covered peak far to the south of his mountain home. But as he crested a sharp ridge he turned and saw, stretching out before him, a barren and desolate plain.

Aramus hesitated upon the ridge, his shaggy coat waving in the cold breeze, and recognized the plain from an earlier time in his life. He studied the land, face hardening with painful memories, but he perceived no movement in the desolation; the land was as empty and lifeless as it had ever been.

Some wounds heal slowly, he thought.

Motionless, Aramus stood on the ridge, his silver shape etched against the golden glow of dawn, and gazed quietly toward the haunting, half-hidden shadow dominating the horizon. Obscured by clouds and a winter haze, the Abyss was almost lost against the skyline, but he could still discern its towering shape.

Aramus smiled faintly as he searched out the mountain in the white mist, for never again had the Dark Council risen from the land, its power crushed completely in that last, great battle. But as Aramus continued to gaze at the Abyss, a disturbing premonition began to settle upon his heart, a strange uneasiness that resurrected ancient ghosts. And a curious need slowly grew within him, a need to know, to be sure. . . .

Only a moment did Aramus hesitate, and when he moved again he was descending the ridge, toward the barren plain. In time he reached level ground and eased into a loping run that carried him purposefully across the desolation. Behind him the sun rose above the horizon, chasing shadows from the land, but Aramus continued to move steadily forward, driven onward by his questioning heart.

And through the day he ran, moving tirelessly and relentlessly over stream and ridge and field until at last he began to ascend the mountain. Yet, still, he did not rest, did not slow his gait until he reached the icy trail and ascended the path, finally emerging upon the summit to stand boldly before the cavern.

Deep in shadow, the sepulchral entrance remained thick with the darkness that had long ago ruled its depths. Aramus peered into the gloom and sniffed, but he could detect no presence. Nervously, he turned his head toward the descending sun, sharply aware of the shadows and chill that embraced him, and his courage

wavered. But he had to know. And with an effort of
will he moved carefully forward, stepping through the
foreboding entrance to be submerged by the gloom.

Alert, he eased cautiously down the darkened,
subterranean tunnel, searching for a threat, but he
sensed nothing living about him. There was only a
strong scent of decay overpowering the dusty air, and
within that scent, a devastating defeat. Moving steadily
and silently Aramus continued forward until he stood
within the main hall, the throne room of Corbis.

Ghastly in the pale light, the cavern floor gleamed
like an ancient grave, scattered with bones of the long
dead. But those were not the bones Aramus sought. And
he moved across the chamber, threading a silent path
through the ghostly remains.

Upon reaching the throne he mounted the steps, his
fear gathering with each stride, until he leaped lightly
past the final stone to land fully upon the blackened
granite, finding his answer at last.

Even more terrifying in death, the skeleton of Corbis
stretched possessively across the throne. Titanic and
spectral, the massive bones shone dully in the frosty
light, fangs still fixed in a frozen roar. But the eyes were
filled only with shadow, void of the fire that had filled
them in life.

Aramus stood quietly over the immense shape and
saw that the bones were dry and pitted, unnaturally
ancient with decay. And he remembered what colossal
strength, what proud might and irresistible will the beast
had commanded while alive. But that great strength

meant nothing now, crushed by a power that ruled the living and the dead.

A soft wind stirred in the chamber and Aramus lifted his head, listening. Then the wind rushed past him and Aramus listened closer, his heart rising to memories of heroes, of courage and love and faith that conquered kingdoms. And Aramus looked down again, silver eyes casting their own light from within, even as the wind swept across the throne, shifting the bones that fell, shattering, crumbling into dust.

Acknowledgments

My greatest debt of gratitude is extended to our merciful and loving heavenly Father, who is always faithful to guide and bless those who strive to serve Him.

I thank Phillip Zodhiates, of GlobaLink, Charlottesville, Virginia, for being the kind of genuine Christian friend that everyone should know at least once in their life. I thank him for his encouragement and for not giving up on seeing the manuscript published after I had abandoned all hope.

And I thank Bill Jensen of Harvest House for his steadfast friendship, for his patience, for believing that *A Wolf Story* was worthy of publication, and for all the selfless assistance he provided to both me and my family.

Others I wish to thank include Scott Allen Morris, whose editing skills in early versions made the book much more than I had conceived. And I thank Judith Markham for her patience and for her exacting craftsmanship in editing the final draft.

Also, I thank Phillip Parker, Texe Marrs, and David Dunham for their support. Each man encouraged me at a different age of my life, and I remain grateful.

And last, and most important of all, I want to thank my Aunt, Bee Nelson. Long years have passed since we sat together beneath the shade trees, but sometimes her words return to me. They were casual words, spoken often, and I failed to understand the wisdom of them at the time. It would only be years later, when I finally turned and looked down the path of my life, that I would finally understand what she had understood from the very beginning when she would come to me, with the faintest smile, and say,

"Sit down, child, and read to me what you wrote today."